Alexander Schmorell
Saint of the German Resistance

Elena Perekrestov

T0164203

Holy Trinity Publications
The Printshop of St Job of Pochaev
Holy Trinity Monastery
Jordanville, New York

2017

Printed with the blessing of His Eminence,
Metropolitan Hilarion First Hierarch
of the Russian Orthodox Church Outside of Russia

———————————

Alexander Schmorell: Saint of the German Resistance
© 2017 Elena Perekrestov

PRINTSHOP OF
SAINT JOB OF POCHAEV

An imprint of

HOLY TRINITY PUBLICATIONS
Holy Trinity Monastery
Jordanville, New York 13361-0036
www.holytrinitypublications.com

ISBN: 978-0-88465-421-6 (paperback)
ISBN: 978-0-88465-456-8 (ePub)
ISBN: 978-0-88465-457-5 (Mobipocket)
Library of Congress Control Number 2016962428

Cover Design: James Bozeman

CONTENTS

He endured hatred who did not know how to hate; he was slain impiously who while dying did not fight back.

—St Cyprian of Carthage on Abel,
the first martyr

I leave this life with the knowledge that I have served my deepest conviction and the truth.

—Alexander Schmorell
Letter to his parents on the day of his execution
July 13, 1943

CHAPTER I

Resisting the Dictatorship of Evil

"Our twentieth century," observed Solzhenitsyn in his Nobel Lecture (1970), "has turned out to be more cruel than those preceding it."[1] But, as St Paul says, "where sin abounded, grace abounded much more."[2] It is not surprising, therefore, that the twentieth century contributed a great multitude of saints to the calendar of the Orthodox Church and that the majority of these saints were martyrs. Among these is a radiant soul whose story is as unique as it is inspiring—St Alexander of Munich, whose short but vibrant life came to a martyric end in 1943.

The fact that these twentieth-century martyrs lived at a time so close to ours is both a blessing and a challenge. On the one hand, the availability of letters, diaries, reminiscences, and official documents allows us to form a picture of a person's disposition and the circumstances of his or her life and death that is much more detailed and comprehensive than we can reconstruct for saints of earlier ages. On the other hand, we are challenged to come to terms with the fact that these saints are people who were much like ourselves, who lived lives so much like ours, and dressed in the familiar attire of the twentieth century instead of the robes more commonly seen in the saints depicted on our icons.

The perplexity that this evokes in us is echoed by a friend of St Alexander, who commented on the fact of his glorification by the Russian Orthodox Church in 2012 by saying, "He would have laughed out loud if he'd known. He wasn't a saint—he was just a normal person."[3]

Just a normal person. How is it that this normal, life-loving young man chose to embark on a course of action that he knew would put his life in jeopardy, and then ultimately came to sacrifice his life? What prompted and, more important, what enabled him, together with a group of close friends (the circle of young students at the University of Munich known to the world now as the White Rose), to bear witness as profoundly believing Christians to their convictions and culture, which were being systematically and brutally annihilated by the Nazis? What gave Alexander and his friends the strength to exhort their fellow Germans to join them in opposing the Nazi regime, which had opposed itself to the Divine Order, and, in so doing, to be among the first to "make the voice of resistance audible in Hitler's Germany"?[4]

And—can a normal, ordinary person indeed be a saint?

Before attempting to answer these questions, we must first recall the backdrop against which the story of the noble and courageous quest of Alexander Schmorell and his circle of friends unfolded.

With Adolph Hitler's rise to power and subsequent imposition of National Socialism throughout all spheres of life in Germany, some people felt compelled (many of them by their Christian faith) to oppose the incursions into their lives and values of a system that sought to control, dominate, and ultimately destroy everything in which they believed. Germany had become a place where "one could no longer speak as one's heart and mind dictated; in which wrong could no longer be called wrong, falsehood could no longer be called falsehood."[5]

Although resistance to the Nazi regime within Germany was not a mass movement, opponents of National Socialism included people from all walks of life and of different convictions: monarchists, Communists, Protestant and Catholic clergy, farmers, aristocrats, students, and army generals. Resistance was based on political, moral, and religious principles.

For some, opposition meant an inner aversion and rejection of Nazism, which could spill over into overt gestures: using *Grüss Gott* (may God greet you), the customary south German greeting, instead of the prescribed *Heil Hitler*, or criticism of the Führer voiced within a close circle of friends. Others were moved to express their opposition to the regime in a more consistent and definitive manner. Such resistance ranged from the actions of isolated individuals who defied Nazi laws and policies, and acted according to their consciences instead,[6] to intricate conspiracies such as the unsuccessful coup d'état and attempt to assassinate Hitler on July 20, 1944, known as Operation Valkyrie.

In both passive and active resistance to Nazism, Christian ideals and idealism played a significant role.[7] In breaking up the structures and sensibilities of old Germany, Hitler and the Nazi Party progressed from covert to overt antagonism to Christianity, using a variety of methods to attack and obliterate it. Far from being purely a political ideology, National Socialism was, in Hitler's own words, "a form of conversion, a new faith."[8] Accordingly, he would stamp out Christianity in Germany, because "one is either a Christian or a German. You can't be both."[9]

Measures to subordinate and then eradicate Christianity included the closure of monasteries, convents, and religious schools; prohibitions against pilgrimages and religious processions; hate and slur campaigns against clergymen; arrests, incarceration, and execution of religious opponents of the regime; along with attempts to bring the Protestant and Roman Catholic Churches under the authority and influence of the state and to institute a Nazi-controlled Protestant state church, known colloquially as the Reich Church.

As part of their program to root out the influence of Christianity, the Nazis took steps to establish a new cult, a "new form" (in reality, a parody) of Christianity, called "Positive Christianity." This was to be a more "heroic" religion than Christianity, with its "enfeebling" preoccupation with sin, mercy, and condescension for the weak. It would be purged of its Old Testament ("Jewish") elements, just as German society would be purged of Jews. Christ was believed to be not a Semite, but an Aryan hero.

Alternative—essentially neopagan—ceremonies for weddings and burials were developed. Christmas festivities were transformed into celebrations of the winter solstice. The swastika (in German—*Hakenkreuz*, meaning "hooked, broken, or twisted cross") was forcibly substituted for the crucifix and religious images in schools and public places.

The Nazi ritual of harvest thanksgiving included the recital of the following "creed" of this new *ersatz* religion:

> *I believe in the land of all the Germans, in a life of service to this land; I believe in the revelation of the Divine creative power and the pure Blood shed in war and peace by the sons of the German National Community, buried in the soil thereby sanctified, risen and living in all for whom it is immolated. I believe in an eternal life on earth of this Blood that was poured out and rose again in all who have recognized the meaning of the sacrifices and are ready to submit to them. . . . Thus I believe in an eternal God, an eternal Germany, and an eternal life.*[10]

Additionally, Nazi "prayers," such as this one, were recited by children at a Nazi-run orphanage:

> *O Führer, my Führer, sent to me by God*
> *Protect and maintain my life*
> *Thou who has served Germany in its hour of need*
> *I thank thee now for my daily bread*
> *Oh! Stay with me, Oh! Never leave me*
> *O Führer, my Führer, my faith and my light.*[11]

Gaining control over the minds of the rising generation was critical; thus, the Nazis made sure that political indoctrination started at an early age. To this end, religious (predominantly Catholic) youth groups and organizations were dissolved and mandatory participation in the Hitler Youth was instituted. Meetings of the Hitler Youth were conducted on Sunday mornings and included the singing of blasphemous songs. Initiation ceremonies into the organization were scheduled at Whitsun to conflict with Catholic confirmation services.

In opposition to Hitler's Reich Church, a church structure known as the Confessing Church arose within the ranks of Protestant clergy and lay people. Well-known members of the Confessing Church were Martin Niemöller and Dietrich Bonhoeffer.[12] When in 1934 a statement was read from Confessing Church pulpits declaring that the church owed its allegiance not to a worldly leader (*Führer*), but to God and Scripture, the Nazis retaliated with arrests and incarcerations.

On Palm Sunday 1937, the priests of all Catholic parishes in Germany read the papal encyclical *Mit brennender Sorge* (With burning concern). It had been smuggled into Germany and printed clandestinely by Catholic presses. In this encyclical, Pope Pius XI expressed his condemnation of the Nazis' racial doctrines, neopaganism, idolatrous cult of state, and blasphemous attitude toward the Old Testament. Reprisals were immediate: trials of Catholic clergy on trumped-up charges of immorality were held, and Catholic printing presses and diocesan publications were shut down.

It wasn't only members of the clergy who recognized the Nazi regime as a manifestation of evil. Many of those who resisted the Nazis or plotted against Hitler and sought to overthrow him did so because they felt that he was destroying Germany morally and spiritually.

Count Helmuth James von Moltke, an officer in the *Abwehr* (German military intelligence service) wrote in 1942:

> An active part of the German people are beginning to realize, not that they have been led astray, not that bad times await them, not that the war may end in defeat, but that what is happening is sin and that they are personally responsible for each terrible deed that has been committed—naturally, not in the earthly sense, but as Christians.[13]

Von Moltke was a member of the clandestine Kreisau Circle, a group of intellectuals who gathered to discuss preparations for the rebirth and restructuring of Germany based on Christian ideals after the downfall of Hitler and National Socialism, which they perceived to be inevitable. This restoration would rectify not only the physical, social, and political devastation of Germany but also the damage that had been inflicted upon the souls, minds, and hearts of the German people. Accused of treason, von Moltke and other members of his circle were arrested and executed.

Among the youth of Germany, a number of groups arose that expressed their opposition to the Third Reich. Working-class teenagers in the industrial areas of Germany banded together into cliques or gangs that called themselves the Edelweiss Pirates (*Edelweisspiraten*). They resented the coercion and paramilitary discipline of the Hitler Youth and preferred to spend their free time as they saw fit. At times, they clashed openly with the leaders of the Hitler Youth, attacking and terrorizing them. During the war, some became more militant and sabotaged government installations, hid deserters, or murdered members of the Gestapo.

Middle- and upper-middle-class youth rebelled against Nazi cultural restrictions by congregating in clubs where they listened and danced to American-style jazz, which was condemned by the Nazis as decadent and associated with a "racially inferior" provenance. The Swing Youth (*Swing Jugend*), as they were known, greeted each other with the words "Swing heil!"

and emulated British and American film stars in their dress.

The Gestapo cracked down on both groups and hundreds were sent to jail or juvenile concentration camps. Some of the more militant resisters paid for their opposition with their lives.[14]

A group of friends, students at the University of Munich, were impelled by their high ideals and Christian consciences to pit themselves against the tyranny of National Socialism. They felt that, by seeking to dominate the entire person through coercion and terror, National Socialism was robbing Germany of its spiritual freedom. Moreover, it grieved them to see that the Third Reich was sacrificing thousands of lives in a senseless war. Calling themselves the White Rose, the students clandestinely wrote and, in the face of terrible danger, distributed throughout several cities six bold and eloquent leaflets exhorting Germans to abandon their apathy, to offer resistance to the insidious oppression of Hitler's regime, and, in so doing, to "fulfill their responsibility as members of Christian and Western civilization."[15] Together with one of their professors, five students, ranging in age from twenty-one to twenty-five years old,[16] were sentenced to death and executed by guillotine in 1943.[17] Among them was a young man of the Russian Orthodox faith, Alexander Schmorell, who was glorified among the saints as a martyr in 2012 by the Russian Orthodox Church.

CHAPTER 2

I Am Orthodox:
We Do It Differently

Alexander Schmorell was born in the city of Orenburg on the Ural River in southern Russia on September 16, 1917[18] scarcely a few weeks before the beginning of the Bolshevik Revolution that would turn the life of his family and country upside down.[19]

Alexander's father, Hugo Schmorell, was a German whose father, Karl-August Schmorell, had come to Russia from East Prussia in the mid-nineteenth century and engaged in commerce, owning a fur shop and the first steam-powered lumber mill in Orenburg. Like other German merchants plying their trade in the city, Karl-August was a well-respected member of Orenburg society, but he retained his German citizenship and his Protestant faith.

Hugo Schmorell was brought up Protestant. When the time came for him to enter university, he went first to Moscow where he studied botany, and then to Munich to study medicine. Upon completing his medical studies in 1907, he returned to Russia to practice as a doctor. There he met and married a Russian woman, Natalia Petrovna Vvedenskaia, who was twelve years his junior.[20] Their wedding took place in the Russian Orthodox Church of Sts Peter and Paul in Orenburg in November 1916. A year later, their newborn son, Alexander, was baptized into the Orthodox faith in the same church.

World War I, the Russian Revolution, and resulting civil war brought the family many trials. Dr Hugo Schmorell was assigned to head a hospital for German prisoners of war in Orenburg. During an outbreak of typhus in the city, Natalia fell ill and died, leaving Alexander, who was about a year old, motherless. Dr Schmorell hired a nanny, a peasant woman named Feodosia Konstantinovna Lapschina, who was to stay with the family until the end of her days more than forty years later.

In 1920, Hugo remarried. His new wife, Elisabeth Hoffman, was, like him, a Russian-born German. Her father owned a brewery in Orenburg.

During the Russian Civil War, Orenburg changed hands several times. With the final entrenchment of the Bolsheviks and the attendant confiscations and oppression, the Schmorell family fled Russia in 1921, when Alexander was not quite four years old. They took up residence in Munich in a comfortable house that was acquired for them by a well-to-do relative. Dr Schmorell succeeded in establishing a medical practice.

Feodosia Lapschina, known to all as simply "Nyanya" (nanny), accompanied the family into exile. To facilitate her departure from Russia and the Soviet authorities, she traveled under the name of Franziska Schmorell, ostensibly the widow of Hugo's deceased brother.[21]

In Munich, the family retained their customary way of life, drinking tea from a samovar, eating traditional Russian dishes (cooked by Nyanya) such as *pelmeni* and *blinchiki*. Russian was spoken in the home. Nyanya never learned more than a few words of German.

Two children, Erich and Natasha, were born to Hugo and Elisabeth in Munich. They too were brought up speaking Russian. Like their mother, they were baptized Roman Catholic. Nevertheless, Elisabeth did her best to ensure that Alexander's religious upbringing was Orthodox. She invited a Russian Orthodox priest into the home for lessons in the Law of God, as Christian instruction in the Russian Orthodox tradition is commonly known.

But it was Alexander's pious nanny who truly nurtured Orthodoxy in him,[22] as well as a love for Russia, the homeland they both had lost. Together they regularly attended services at the Russian Orthodox parish in Munich—Nyanya dressed, as always, in her wide peasant skirts and ever-present kerchief. During Orthodox fasting periods, she would prepare Lenten dishes for the two of them, while she served the rest of the family their usual fare.[23]

Nyanya's love of Russian folksongs infected the whole family; she sang lullabies to the children at night and accompanied her cooking with song. Nyanya knew many Russian folk tales. She told the children stories of life in her village in Russia, and of Stenka Razin, leader of several Cossack rebellions in seventeenth-century Russia whose daring exploits had become legendary, and whom Nyanya claimed as an ancestor. And, most important, she told Shurik (as Alexander was called by his family and his Russian friends) all about his mother, whom he could scarcely remember.

The family atmosphere was warm and amicable. The parents, especially Alexander's father, had broad cultural interests. They cultivated in Alexander a love for art, music, and literature. A piano was purchased and rapidly became an integral part of the Schmorell home. The children all took lessons, and even though Alexander always found things more important than practicing piano to occupy himself with, he played beautifully. The family library contained the collected works of Pushkin, Chekhov, Turgenev, Tolstoy, and Dostoyevsky. The children read the Russian classics in the original. Alexander had lessons in English conversation from an Englishwoman. From his father, who had set up a workshop in the Schmorell basement, Alexander learned the crafts of bookbinding and carpentry, and he came to enjoy the process of working with his hands.

Hugo's stories about Russia, of his happy childhood and youth in prerevolutionary times, complemented Nyanya's and helped to shape Alexander's perception of his lost homeland—a Russia that had been destroyed by Bolshevism and the chaos of revolution—and gave rise to a love and longing for this Russia and its ideals.

One story, which Shurik heard from his father when he was already an adult, made an indelible impression on him. He was moved to recount it in a letter to a friend: "Last night … Father told me a powerful story that affected me intensely." The account was of the death of Admiral Kolchak, leader of the anti-Bolshevik White forces during the civil war that had ensued in Russia after the Revolution of 1917.

> He fell into the hands of the Reds [Bolsheviks] and was to be shot. But at his execution he comported himself so nobly, that the Red soldiers … who were supposed to shoot him, refused to fire! And then—and here comes one of the most phenomenal things I have ever heard—Kolchak gives them the order to shoot!!! Only then did they fire. . . . What a man he must have been—what tremendous strength![24]

The hospitable Schmorell home attracted a wide and varied circle of visitors and friends—artists, writers, musicians, medical professionals, and Orthodox clergymen—many of whom were Russian exiles. Among these was the family of Leonid Pasternak, a post-Impressionist Russian painter, whose wife, Rosalia Kaufman, was a well-known pianist from Moscow.[25] Leonid gave the family a sketch he had made of Beethoven. Later, when Shurik took up sculpting, he created a bust of Beethoven, his favorite composer, from this sketch.

The Schmorells extended their hospitality and aid to displaced Russians who found themselves in difficult circumstances. One Russian young woman, who came to Munich from Yugoslavia in the early 1940s, stayed with the Schmorells until she could find a job and a place to live. She came back for a visit to the Schmorell house one evening to spend time with the younger Schmorells. Upon seeing her, Dr Schmorell inquired in a concerned manner why she looked so forlorn. She answered that she was tired of always being hungry. Dr Schmorell commiserated with her, then asked what she would like to eat if she could get anything she wanted. Her spontaneous answer was "duck!" When she was invited to dinner at the Schmorell house a few weeks later, to her great delight and surprise (it was, after all, wartime Germany) she was served … duck.[26]

Nyanya contributed to the family's efforts in aiding needy Russians. In 1941, a young woman of seventeen was brought from German-occupied Rostov to work in a Munich factory. She met Alexander one Sunday when they both happened to be on the same tram on their way to church. When they arrived, they met Nyanya there, and Alexander introduced his new acquaintance to her. Later on, during one of her visits to the Schmorell home, the young woman received a much-appreciated gift from Nyanya—a roll of dotted white calico for a new dress.[27]

We find mention of another of Nyanya's charitable deeds in a letter written by Alexander during the bleak winter of late 1942. Munich had received a new wave of Russian forced laborers who were suffering want and hardships. Alexander tells his correspondent that, as he is writing, "Nyanya is sitting at my side, knitting gloves for Russians."[28]

At age seven, Alexander was enrolled in a private elementary school, and at ten in the Wilhelmsgymnasium. This was Munich's oldest secondary school, founded in 1559, where education was focused on the study of the humanities and classics, including the study of Ancient Greek and Latin. According to a teacher's remarks at this time, Alexander was well behaved and good natured, physically strong, with good endurance. He appeared shy and inhibited. Perhaps, the teacher surmised, Alexander felt somewhat out of place among his classmates because of his background. However, he was known to fool around on occasion. He did well in most subjects and excelled in drawing; but in geography, the teacher noted, he could be more diligent.

One year, his Latin teacher did not pass him. Alexander's half-brother, Erich, recalled that his mother had the impression that the Latin teacher had failed Alexander not on account of unsatisfactory knowledge, but rather because of an aversion to his half-Russian descent and his Russian Orthodox religion.

Alexander was transferred to another school, the Neue Realgymnasium, where he stayed until his *Abitur*[29] in 1937. The headmaster of this school was characterized as one of the most upright men of his time. He steadfastly refused to join the Nazi Party after the takeover in 1933 and was not inclined to force his students to enter the Hitler Youth. In 1937, the year of Alexander's *Abitur*, the headmaster was transferred to another school and demoted to the position of senior teacher because of his uncompromising Christian attitude.

At the Neue Realgymnasium, Alexander's grades were rather good, though his attitude toward school was noted as being at times a bit casual. A schoolmate from this time described Alexander as "good-looking, athletic, kind."

The same schoolfellow reported the following: "For religious instruction, he [Schmorell] joined us Catholics.[30] Several times Professor Westermaier said: 'Schmorell, as our guest you could make the sign of the cross as we do—from left to right.' But he would always answer: 'I am Orthodox. We do it differently.' And that's how it stayed."[31]

At least in this respect, it seems that Alexander was able to overcome his shyness. He had come to terms with being different from his schoolmates and expected others to accept it as well.

CHAPTER 3

Facing Man's Cruel Handiwork

At the Neue Realgymnasium, Alexander met and became good friends with Christoph Probst, a fellow student. This was a deep friendship that lasted until Christoph was executed, together with the siblings Hans and Sophie Scholl, after the first White Rose trial. In the Probst household, Alexander encountered an openness and respect for other cultures and religions.[32] The children were brought up vaguely Christian, but with no particular faith, although later in life Christoph was drawn toward Catholicism.

Perhaps it was this atmosphere of openness that made Alexander feel less of an outsider. Be that as it may, the two boys developed a friendship that gave Alexander "self-awareness, self-confidence and joy of life."[33] In turn, Christoph sought out Alexander's company because, as he wrote to his stepmother, "with him around, you don't feel any agitation or frustration; he only raises the mood."[34] The two shared many interests. Together they built a plankton aquarium and studied it under a microscope. They enjoyed the outdoors together—hiking, skiing, mountain climbing, swimming. When they were older, they both took up fencing.

Christoph had an older sister, Angelika, with whom Alexander became fast friends, and who shared his love of horses. Years later, Angelika was to describe her first meeting with Alexander, which took place shortly before his eighteenth birthday (she was seventeen at the time). Christoph and Alexander had gone horseback riding, and Angelika was invited to join them. "It was a cloudy fall day. Alex rode among the other riders like a young prince and surpassed the others in good looks and confidence of bearing. Something radiant, triumphant emanated from his tall, slim figure, his gold-blond hair, and laughing mouth."[35]

Traute Lafrenz, a young medical student whom Alexander met when he went to study at the university in Hamburg, reminisced that "he was a tall young man, with a large mouth, full of enthusiasm, and when he laughed the sun came out."[36] Yet another friend characterized him as "a person with a wondrous—laughing, radiant—soul in his luminous eyes."[37]

"There can be few men who had Alex's radiant, relaxed humor," wrote Inge Scholl, sister of Hans and Sophie.

> He beheld the world with eyes full of imagination—it was as if he saw it anew each day. He found the world beautiful, fresh, and filled with captivating delights, and he enjoyed it in an open, childlike way, without questioning or calculating. He was at once totally receptive and unstintingly generous, dispensing gifts royally. Sometimes, however, there appeared behind his cheerful, untrammeled manner something else—a questioning and seeking, an ancient, deep-seated seriousness.[38]

Alexander loved nature and liked to wander around the countryside alone, with no particular destination in mind. He would strike up conversations with tramps, farmhands, beggars, and gypsies and marvel at the interesting things they said, relating these to his friends in conversation the next day. Perhaps his affinity for these people stemmed from a disinclination to subject his freedom-loving soul to the ever-increasing enforced homogeneity of German society under the Nazis. It may be that he felt more at home among people outside conventional or mainstream society. "From my earliest youth, I was incredibly shy," he divulged in a letter to Angelika, "especially with respect to relatives and friends. Everything I did … was my secret; no one was supposed to see. . . . I did everything not for the sake of others, but for its own sake, for the sake of a purpose that I always perceived perfectly clearly in my heart."[39]

Determination and perseverance were part of the fabric of Alexander's character. His brother Erich recalled a two-week family summer vacation at a lake. The family had rented rooms in a hotel, but Alexander refused to sleep inside. He pitched a small tent next to the hotel. Unfortunately, it rained hard for most of the two weeks, but Alexander didn't give up. He slept in the tent, after digging ditches around it to divert the rainwater.

Partly out of his love for nature, partly from a desire for adventure, Alexander enrolled in a youth league while still in secondary school, going with them on hikes and bike trips. When this organization was absorbed into the Hitler Youth, Alexander resented the regimentation and unquestioning obedience required of him, stopped attending meetings, and finally withdrew his membership.

Although his parents were apolitical, they were nevertheless extremely skeptical about National Socialism. His stepmother was especially vocal in her criticism of Hitler. Thus, the adults of his household echoed, and likely fostered, Alexander's fledgling aversion to the new regime, which had arisen out of his experiences with the Hitler Youth and out of his reaction to such events as the "Night of the Long Knives," Hitler's bloody purge of his opponents in the Nazi Party in the summer of 1934.

In 1937, upon passing his *Abitur*, Alexander was required to put in time with the *Reichsarbeitsdienst* (National Labor Service). He was sent to work on road construction in southern Germany, where he lived in a camp with other young men who were serving their time of compulsory service. The monotony of the work, the regimented life in the camp with its lack of freedom and free time, the knowledge that his letters were liable to be opened and read by a camp censor, and the daily dose of National Socialist indoctrination—all of this was oppressive. This induced him to write in a letter that he was able to post outside the camp: "Nothing is greater than freedom of thought and independence of one's own will—when one does not fear these. Here they try to rob you of them, to make you forget them, or sever you from them, but in this they will not succeed."[40]

After his six months in the *Reichsarbeitsdienst* were up, it was the army's turn to claim Alexander for compulsory service. His love for horses and riding led him to enlist in the cavalry. But when he was forced to swear the obligatory oath of loyalty to Hitler, his conscience was so perturbed at the thought of wearing a German uniform while holding sympathies with his native Russia[41] that he informed his superiors of this conflict of loyalties and asked to be discharged from the army. His request was turned down, but, strangely, he suffered no consequences (although his father was called in for a conference).

With his cavalry unit, in 1938, Alexander experienced the annexation of Austria and the occupation of the Sudetenland (the border regions of Czechoslovakia inhabited by ethnic Germans). There he became a witness to cruelties that horrified him, and he saw that reality (resistance to the occupation) did not correspond to what Nazi propaganda presented in the media (unmitigated joy of the local population at reunification).

In March 1939, Alexander was released from his compulsory service in the army. It soon became apparent, however, that war was imminent. Alexander had dreamed of entering a profession somehow related to the arts, but now his father convinced him to follow in his own footsteps and study medicine. Alexander, who had come to loathe the military, was attracted by the idea that in case of mobilization, medical personnel would not be forced to fight (i.e., to *kill*) but instead would serve their fellow men and *save lives*. He entered medical school, first in Hamburg, and then at the University of Munich, where his father had studied medicine. There he was joined in his studies by Christoph Probst.

On September 1, 1939, Hitler invaded Poland, precipitating World War II. And thus, "the war within the country, against single individuals, turned into the war against the nations."[42] Britain and France responded to the German invasion of Poland with a declaration of war on September 3, but no concrete aid to the Poles was forthcoming. On May 10, 1940, German forces invaded Belgium, the Netherlands, and Luxembourg, and rapidly pushed on into France. The French signed an armistice on June 22, and Nazi forces occupied a large part of the country.

Alexander was conscripted in April 1940, and in May, he was sent with a medical unit to newly occupied France.

The suffering he saw, inflicted on both sides during the fighting, gave Alexander cause to despise the National Socialist government of Germany even more than before.

Never one to spend time aimlessly, Alexander used his free time in France to pursue his own interests. He practiced playing the organ in a local church at times when no services were being held. He indulged in his love of reading, and especially of Russian literature. The books he read were sent in a steady stream by Alexander's parents at his request. He translated a story by Chekhov into German and sent it to Angelika Probst.

Returning to Munich in the fall of 1940, Alexander resumed his medical studies at the University of Munich. As a student-soldier, he was also assigned to the medical unit of the Second Student-Military Company as an army medic. He was required to wear the uniform of the German army; to show up periodically for drills, marches, and ideological speeches; and to put in several hours of work per week in military hospitals, taking care of the wounded. Student medical companies were a haven for young men who dissented with National Socialism, had qualms about fighting for the Nazi regime, and had entered the study of medicine to avoid active combat duty. It was in this medical company that Alexander met Hans Scholl, with whom he would soon form the nucleus of resistance activities. They saw eye-to-eye on the military and on the Nazis, and found this stage in their own lives "absurd and barbaric."[43] They avoided wearing their uniforms whenever possible and would periodically slip away from the company's required musters, bringing with them a good book to read in a field somewhere out of sight of their superiors.

One of the books that Alexander and Hans read on such an occasion was an edition of Rodin's sculptures. Perusal of the works in this album, wrote Alexander to Angelika,

> lifted the veil that so often exists between you and such glorious creations; everything becomes so clear, you sense the creator's intention, and then you apprehend this incredible beauty which makes you tremble. Do you ever get this trembling when listening to Beethoven, Tchaikovsky? Or when you stand in front of a Michelangelo, a Rodin or a Phidias?[44]

Art, music, and literature were interests that Alexander and Hans shared, in which they sought sanctuary, and that provided their inner lives with uplifting sustenance. Reading the poetry of Hermann Hesse and Rainer Maria Rilke furnished them with penetrating thoughts couched in strikingly worded utterances that could be easily memorized and held onto for moral support. Together the two friends would attend concerts of classical music, and Alexander would leave the concert hall inspired and motivated to take up his piano playing once more. He played Tchaikovsky well, and would abandon himself without restraint to the elemental power of Beethoven's music. Yet he could be equally enthralled by the sense of discipline and divine order that Bach's fugues exuded. In his estimation, "Bach's music can be defined as the desire to serve God in perpetually onward-flowing, unending worship of the Most High."[45]

Like Alexander, Hans experienced Christianity not as a relic of the past, but as a living faith. His mother, who had been a lay deaconess before her marriage, brought him up as a pious Protestant. Hans's letters and especially his diary reflect his spiritual quest and his belief that truth will ultimately triumph. "Spiritual nihilism," he wrote, "was a major threat to European civilization … [yet] all values can never be destroyed among all men. There still exist custodians who will kindle the flame and pass it from hand to hand until a new wave of rebirth inundates the land."[46]

Hans had come to realize the incompatibility of his ideals with those of the Nazi state. As a boy he had joined the Hitler Youth in wide-eyed idealism—against the wishes of his father, who was critical of Hitler and the Nazis. A series of incidents had disillusioned Hans,[47] so he withdrew from the movement and instead joined with an independent youth group called *dj.1.11*.[48]

In 1936, all youth groups other than the Hitler Youth were banned. A year later, the Nazis cracked down on anyone still daring to cling to membership in these outlawed groups. These were youth who resisted being forced into a mold and engaged in activities frowned upon by the Nazis: playing non-German instruments such as the banjo and balalaika; singing foreign folk music— Balkan ballads, Cossack songs, and American cowboy tunes; and telling forbidden jokes. Instead of drilling, marching, and saluting, these young people communed with nature, wrote poetry, and engaged in thoughtful discussions about life and God. During this crackdown, many young people were arrested and interrogated, including Hans and Sophie Scholl and two of their siblings.

Neither Hans nor Alexander were made of stuff that yielded readily to the enforced conformity of Nazi *Gleichschaltung*—the policy of bringing all aspects of German society into total coordination with National Socialist ideology. Hans, like Alexander, had been sent to France in 1940 where he was faced with the ugliness of war, with death. "War sets us back a long way," he wrote to his sister Inge. "It's unbelievable how absurd human beings have become."[49] Two years further into the war, he would write in his diary: "O God of love, help me to overcome my doubts. I see the Creation, Your handiwork, which is good. But I also see man's handiwork, our handiwork, which is cruel."[50]

Life posed questions that were not easy to answer.

Upon his return from France in the fall of 1940, Alexander resumed his usual attendance of services at the Russian Orthodox Church in Munich. At this time, the Russian émigré community in Munich had grown, owing to a large number of Russians who had recently arrived from France. Having occupied France, the Germans demanded that the French authorities send people to work in Germany. Russian émigrés living in France—people who had already been forced to flee their homeland once—were prime candidates for this work. French officials entered their names into the lists of those who were to be sent away—to lose their homes one more time.

Seeing these unfortunates in church, Alexander's heart bled. One Sunday in spring, he gave vent to his empathetic anguish in a letter: "These were all people who had once left their homeland in order to escape bondage, in order not to have to serve a hated idea." He wrote:

> They fled to save their own and their children's freedom. . . . With great effort they acquired modest, humble homes in France. Then a terribly cruel fate drove them away, yet again, to a foreign land. They've been praying for twenty-two years. And now, when they've been displaced for the second time, they still believe, they all still come to church, and pray and hope.[51]

But that wasn't all that disquieted him. On his way to church, he had seen people lining up for the movie theaters—and this was Easter day for the Western Christians. Alexander articluated his indignation and resentment:

> Why do those wretched creatures have work, bread, a home, a homeland, and why do those people whom I saw in church lack these things? … And yet they pray and believe. Isn't belief

then the most important thing? … I stood in a dark corner, saw all these unfortunates, and tears streamed down my cheeks. I was not ashamed of them.[52]

Alexander's empathy with those whose lives had been ravaged by the war began to spill into action. French prisoners of war had been streaming into a prisoner-of-war camp in the environs of Munich. "Alexander would collect whatever bread and cigarettes he could get his hands on," remembers his friend Nikolai Hamazaspian,[53] "and we would bring all this to the camp on our bicycles."[54] Later, after June 1941, when the Third Reich declared war on the Soviet Union, and Russian prisoners of war and forced laborers began to arrive in Germany, this scenario would be repeated.[55]

CHAPTER 4

Coming Together

The circle of friends grew wider. Alexander introduced Hans to Christoph Probst, who had married and become a father (the only student member of the White Rose circle who was a family man). Christoph's inclination to reflect on things spiritual had led to a steadily deepening relationship with Christianity, partly under the influence of his father-in-law, Harald Dohrn, a profoundly religious man and convinced anti-Nazi.[56] At the same time, Christoph had come to a more acute rejection of National Socialism, which he said was "the name of a malignant spiritual disease that has befallen our people."[57]

Another medical student who had no sympathy for the National Socialist system, and one of the last to join the group, was Willi Graf.[58] From his early youth, Willi had been a devout Catholic. He had refused to join the

Hitler Youth, preferring membership in the outlawed *Grauer Orden* (Gray Order), a Catholic youth organization that, along with hiking in the outdoors, was interested in reading and discussing theology and liturgical reform.[59] He would cross out from his address book the names of friends who had joined the Hitler Youth, and avoided associating with them thereafter. Like Hans, he had been arrested for his connection with the free youth groups.

Before coming to Munich in the spring of 1942, Willi had been on the Eastern Front and had seen things behind the lines that were "so terrible, I would never have thought them possible. . . . I wish I hadn't had to see what I have seen."[60] He was referring to the horrific brutality with which his fellow soldiers treated civilians in conquered areas.

When he came to Munich from the front, Willi was assigned to the Second Student-Military Company, where he met Alexander and his circle of friends. In Munich Willi was also able to indulge in his interests: fencing, literature, and theology. An avid musician, he joined the Munich Bach Choir.

In a letter to his sister, Willi echoed Alexander's preoccupation with understanding what faith is: "Belief is no simple thing. It demands constant strain and struggle … To be a true Christian … is the most difficult thing of all, because we are never, ever, able to be true Christians— except in death."[61]

His deeply Christian convictions are manifest in a statement that Willi wrote in his death cell, explaining the reason for his rejection of National Socialism: "For us, the people of the Occident, Christianity is the tradition upon which we have built and carry on our spiritual and cultural life. . . . Without religion, a state can have no permanence. All order comes from God, equally for the family, the people, or the state."[62]

As a much-needed refuge from the agonizing realities of wartime existence under the Nazis, Alexander began to immerse himself in art—sculpture and drawing. His first attempt at sculpture, a bust of Beethoven, attempted to convey the composer's passionate and pensive spirit. Inspired by the work of Rodin, Alexander created a study of his nanny's hands that emulated the master's technique. In a drawing class, Alexander met Lilo Ramdohr, who became a close friend. Lilo reminisces that outwardly at this time Alexander would often be in high spirits, which she attributes to his immersion in the creative process. And inwardly, "it seemed to me as if he had probed several degrees deeper into his own nature," she writes.[63]

Perhaps Alexander's state was the reflection of another source of support that he had turned to at this time. Lilo noted that he constantly carried with him a small book, which she thought was a Bible. Alexander's family, however, was of the opinion that it was an Orthodox prayer book.[64] This must have provided another, more profound, haven for him than his art could offer.

But there was a lighter side to Alexander, which Lilo also captured in her memory: "I remember when it rained, we would go walking in the rain, and he would put his collar up, lean backwards, with his mouth open, and let it rain into his mouth. I would say, 'What are you doing? I have an umbrella.' And he would say, 'I just like rainwater.'"[65]

Margaret Knittel, a violinist, provides another glimpse into Alexander's personality as she remembers how she met him for the first time: "I was leaving the store, loaded down with packages; a young man sprang out from behind me and offered to carry everything to my door. It was Alex! I thankfully accepted." As they walked, a lively conversation took place. "The fact that I was studying music at the Mozarteum interested him greatly. . . . Strangely enough, he never betrayed the fact that he played the piano!"[66] Gallantry and modesty seem to have been characteristic of Alexander.

Sophie Scholl was the last member of the core group of the White Rose to arrive in Munich. She was also the youngest (twenty-one years old at the time of her death), and the only woman. She came from Ulm to Munich in May 1942 to study at the university, majoring in biology and philosophy. She soon became an inseparable part of her brother's circle of friends, sharing both their interests and their convictions.

Sophie was not aware of Hans and Alexander's resistance scheme at the time of its inception,[67] but once she found out about the leaflet campaign, she threw herself into the work with the fervor, dedication, and boldness that were so characteristic of her.

Alexander's personality elicited a characterization from Sophie that was evocative of what others had noted: "I can't help but delight in his radiant smile and his child's heart."[68] She was also struck by Alexander's "faith in others coupled with an infinite readiness to help them."[69] Lilo discerned the same quality in him: "It was in Alex's nature to make others happy. For instance, at times he would go a long way round the bombed-out streets of Munch in order to bring me something or to fulfill a wish of mine."[70] In remembering how unconditionally Alexander stood by Hans's side throughout their valiant venture, Lilo extolls Alexander's "capability to regard a friend's concerns as his own, his intense loyalty as a friend, his indescribable capacity for putting himself out for another person."[71]

Like Alexander, Sophie was an artist, and she was asked to illustrate several children's books. She found joy and respite in music. While doing her compulsory war service as a nursery teacher at a school attached to a munitions factory, Sophie heard a composition "by whom, I don't know, but written in the time of Bach." She describes it as a "marvelously lucid, majestic, joyous quartet." It made her long "to breathe the same clear air as those who had created the piece. And that desire proved sufficient to distance me from the turmoil around me, with its resemblance to glutinous, hostile mush."[72]

Although music and the other arts were a haven, a source of consolation that nurtured and uplifted the soul, there was something even higher that the young people aspired to. During a skiing trip, which the friends spent in a hut on a mountain, the question of spiritual hunger had come up. "Most of you will know how grand it is to sit around a stove by candlelight, with a few friends, in the solitude that reigns at 2,000 meters, with wind-driven snow lashing the four walls outside," wrote one of those present. Huddled around the stove, they read psalms, poems of Novalis, and Dostoevsky. "Books lent our days in the hut a very special flavor because they focused everyone's thoughts on the same subjects," and then "one of us brought the conversation around to hunger ... hunger for things of the spirit. . . . Was the wide realm of art, literature and music capable of assuaging spiritual hunger?"[73]

Mulling over this question, Sophie arrived at an answer to which the others would very likely agree: "Can music really satisfy spiritual hunger? Can something that springs from the soul be its food as well? That would be like a body having to construct itself out of itself alone ... While pondering on the hunger that exists in mankind ... I've become aware that we would starve to death if unsustained by God."[74] And thus she turned to God in her diary, pleading:

My soul is like an arid waste when I try to pray to You, conscious of nothing but its own barrenness. My God, transform that ground into good soil so that Your seed doesn't fall on it in vain. . . . Do not turn away from me if I fail to hear You knock; open my deaf, deaf heart. . . . Receive me and do with me as You will, I beseech You, I beseech You.[75]

CHAPTER 5

Books and Mentors

In searching for answers to their deepest questions, Alexander and his circle of friends not infrequently turned to books. It was Alexander who introduced them to the works of Dostoyevsky with their profoundly Christian perception of man, his history and his moral condition. In Dostoyevsky's Grand Inquisitor—his denunciation of Christ, and his proclivity to forcibly make men live "happily," but in ignorance—they saw a reflection of Hitler. So immersed in Dostoyevsky's *Brothers Karamazov* was Alexander, that he even signed some of his letters as "Alyosha," the name of the work's protagonist.[76] The loving and gentle Alyosha Karamazov believes in and searches for truth, and with his entire being, he desires to serve it, to venture for its sake upon a path of ascetic self-denial even to the point of sacrificing his own life.

Periodically, the friends would gather—sometimes just among themselves, sometimes with older like-minded individuals—to read aloud from and discuss literary and philosophical works of special importance to them. These reading evenings, which Alexander called sessions of "spiritual refreshment," were neither an arena for political polemic nor a gathering of conspirators plotting against the regime. They were rather the occasion for intellectual and spiritual probings through which the participants, who felt themselves to be under "spiritual siege,"[77] sought to analyze the devastating chaos of the times and to spiritually fortify themselves against it. Readings were held at various locations, including the Schmorell house and the residence of the elderly scholar and editor Carl Muth (1867–1944).

Muth, a Catholic, had founded and published *Hochland* (Highland), a journal of religion, art, and philosophy. During the Nazi years, the journal had expressed oblique criticism of the regime, usually through articles of an historical nature from which an astute reader could draw parallels to contemporary reality. In June 1941, by order of the Nazis, *Hochland* ceased publication.[78]

Just a few months later, a mutual friend gave Hans Scholl a letter of introduction to Muth. The two instantly took to each other. Soon Muth entrusted Hans Scholl with the task of cataloging his extensive library, which contained many books that were not easily obtainable in Nazi Germany. These books now became accessible not only to

Hans but also to Alexander and Sophie, who also began to frequent Muth's house on the outskirts of Munich. Among Muth's books were the works of contemporary French writers Paul Claudel (1868–1955) and Georges Bernanos (1888–1948). Their reflections on the modern world (which Bernanos saw as a "vast conspiracy against man"[79]) from the vantage point of a conscious Christianity were an invaluable aid to the students in attempting to make sense of a world that seemed to have lost its moorings. In the works of Claudel and Bernanos they also found reassurance. "Life is a great adventure toward the light," wrote Claudel.[80] Although darkness may seem to prevail, "night had to be, that this light might appear."[81]

Muth introduced Alexander and Hans to the archivist of the Monastery of St Boniface in Munich, who opened up the holdings of the monastery library to them, widening the scope of their reading even further. However, it soon became apparent that the library was in danger, as the Nazis were about to shut down the monastery. With the permission of the archivist, Hans and Alexander carried away as many of the library's rare books as they could and took them to the Schmorell house for safekeeping.[82]

Since his youth, Muth had been preoccupied with determining and describing the relationship between the spiritual and the aesthetic. He had come to believe that the purpose of art was essentially religious. Human creativity is a gift from the Creator, and the art that human beings create "should serve to elevate man to God as the highest good. . . . Through the portrayal of beauty, the artist awakens love, namely love for the Divine. . . . Art's purpose is to make mankind receptive to the spiritual through beauty that is perceptible to the senses."[83]

This resonated with the beliefs and interests of the White Rose circle, most of whom were involved intimately with the arts. In turn, Alexander, the Scholls, and their friends were a source of consolation to the elderly Muth: they were tangible proof that not all of Germany's younger generation had been brainwashed and corrupted by the Nazis. A warm and fast friendship grew between the scholar and the students, and Muth's house became a frequent refuge for his young protégés. Here Alexander and his friends encountered theologians, philosophers, and writers whose views were in opposition to the regime; a spiritual and moral assessment of the Nazi phenomenon was a constant subject of conversation.

Through Muth, the young people met Theodor Haecker (1879–1945), an author, scholar, and philosopher (and, like Muth, a Catholic). Perceiving early on the true nature of National Socialism, Haecker had been arrested for expressing his criticism of it in an article published soon after Hitler came to power. He was released but had been forbidden to speak in public since 1935 and to publish his works since 1938.

Invited to reading evenings held by members of the White Rose circle, Haecker read from his unpublished works, including his diaries, entitled *Journal in the Night,* in which he voiced all that he was forbidden to express in print.[84] Haecker believed that for Germany, it had come down to one ultimate choice: "Now it is clearly and evidently a matter of Christ, or anti-Christ [*sic*],"[85] and he maintained that the Nazi swastika was "the emblem of the antichrist."[86] His journal entry for May 12, 1940, reads thus:

> The leadership of Germany today … is consciously anti-Christian. It hates Christ whom it does not name. . . . We Germans are fighting this war on the wrong side! We are, as to the majority, making war as willing slaves, and as to the minority, as the unwilling slaves of a government that has apostatized. . . . The German people will be beaten, but not struck down and wiped out. The one ray of light in my mind is this: it is better for a people to be defeated and to suffer, than to sin and apostatize.[87]

Permeating all Haecker's utterances and actions was the overarching conviction that one ought to obey God rather than men.

Through their conversations and friendship, which stemmed from a solicitous attitude toward the younger generation, the two elderly mentors, Haecker and Muth, confirmed Alexander and his friends in their rejection of the diabolical inhumanity that was being imposed on Germany, and helped the students to clarify and solidify their spiritual resistance to the order of things around them.

In spiritually analyzing the plight of modern man, Muth and Haecker turned at times to the experience of Eastern Christianity[88]—to Russian writers and philosophers.[89] Foremost among these was Dostoyevsky, with his interpretation of the human condition, the possibility he saw of redressing the spiritual nihilism that threatened European civilization, and his belief that the human soul could triumph over darkness—be it imposed from within or from without. A contributor to *Hochland*, German theologian and essayist Karl Pfleger, summarized Dostoevsky thus:

> Dostoevsky, more than … any modern mind gazed … into the dark, irrational abyss of human nature, man's essential possibility of chaos. But he also spoke of "the restoration of ruined man" … with the advent of a new and profound knowledge of redemption, of man's essential union with God, of what the Russian philosophy of religion terms the mystery of Divine humanity.[90]

Another influence on Muth and Haecker was their Russian contemporary, the Christian existentialist philosopher Nikolai Berdyaev, then living in exile in Paris.[91] Several of Berdyaev's books had been translated into German and were read by several members of the White Rose circle. Articles by Berdyaev were published in *Hochland* and his books were reviewed there. Muth and Haecker perceived him as Dostoevsky's heir in exploring the questions of God, human nature, spirituality, history, freedom, and creativity from a Christian standpoint. As someone who had experienced the upheavals (what he called "the vertiginous waves of devastation"[92]) of the twentieth century, the crushing and dehumanizing godless totalitarianism of the Communist system in his native Russia, Berdyaev could offer profound commentary on the epoch in which they all were living—the anti-Christian epoch of Bolshevism and National Socialism.

Berdyaev believed that "the rhythm of history is changing: it is becoming catastrophic." The civilization of Europe is in profound crisis; the bases of her culture are being undermined. "Our time is a time of spiritual decadence," of "withering" and of a "frightening emptiness" which permeates all spheres of modern-day life, not the least of which are the arts. Ever since the Renaissance, European man had been "tearing himself from his religious center, separating himself from the might of God," and in spurning his cornerstone, he falls back into chaos. What does the loss of Christianity mean for Europe? "Man without God is no longer man."

And yet, human nature "has infinite capacity for regeneration and recovery." Like, Dostoyevsky, Berdyaev feels hope for a spiritual rebirth, a Christian renaissance, although "perhaps it will show itself in the catacombs and be welcomed by only a few. Perhaps it will happen only at the end of time. It is not for us to know." Nevertheless, before this renewal can take place, "I have a presentiment that an outbreak of the powers of evil is at hand. . . . The night is coming and we must take up spiritual weapons for the fight against evil, we must make more sensitive our power for its discernment."

Russia, which had already been engulfed by "night," had its spiritual experience to offer to the West: "Persecution has never been any danger to the Christian life … for it actually strengthens and spreads true religious life. . . . Christians have again shown that they know how to die. The Orthodox Church is humbled and brought low from the outside, but within she is enlarged and lifted up in glory: she has her martyrs."

Thus was the worldview of the White Rose circle and their mentors reinforced by the influence of Orthodox thought.

CHAPTER 6

Days of Darkness

The Nazi offensive against Christianity in Germany had meanwhile intensified. Crucifixes were banned from all schools in Bavaria by the local party leader in April 1941. The reaction was quite vehement. Enraged parents petitioned, protested, and even threw out pictures of Hitler that had displaced the crucifixes. As a result, the decree was rescinded.

In the summer of that year, rumors began to circulate about some sinister developments. Inmates of nursing homes, hospitals, and mental wards were beginning to disappear suddenly and inexplicably. A friend of Mrs Scholl who worked in a home for mentally disabled children told her that a convoy of SS trucks had taken the children away.

Such episodes revealed the implementation of *Aktion T4*, the euthanasia program instituted by the Nazis for the purpose of rooting out the "useless" and "unproductive" elements of society—the deformed, the terminally ill, the mentally disabled—in keeping with their racial doctrine. Eventually close to eighty thousand "defective" people were "released" at various "release centers" throughout the Reich.

As more and more "death wagons" wended their way to these centers, the Catholic bishop of Münster, Clemens August von Galen, raised his voice in protest. In the summer of 1941, at the height of Hitler's military victories, he delivered several sermons in which he fervidly protested against the dispersal of religious communities that had recently taken place in his diocese and against the killing of thousands of innocent people. He was outraged by the euthanasia program. It was "against God's commandments, against the law of nature, and against the system of jurisprudence in Germany."[93] Who was safe? Who will be next? he asked. Perhaps the badly wounded and crippled soldiers, rendered "useless" and "unproductive" by their injuries, would find such a "welcome" upon their return home from the front.

Inveighing against the unlawful actions of the Nazi government, von Galen called for the restoration of justice. "If this call remains unheard and unanswered, … then our German people and our country—in spite of the heroism of our soldiers and the glorious victories they have won—will perish through an inner rottenness and decay."[94]

While German soldiers were fighting against an external foe, the bishop warned, there was an "internal enemy [by which he meant the government and its secret police—*EP*] who strikes us and torments us … seeking to reshape our people and even our youth, to turn them away from God." However, as this is an enemy against which "we cannot fight with arms, … [we must] become hard, remain firm, remain steadfast! Like the anvil under the blows of the hammer! It may be that obedience to our God and faithfulness to our conscience may cost me or any of you life, freedom or home. But: 'Better to die than to sin!'"[95]

Though the words of von Galen's sermons were not published in the press, they nevertheless reached far and wide. They were written down, duplicated secretly, and disseminated—passed hand to hand or mailed anonymously—throughout Germany, the occupied territories, and at the front.

Though some in the Nazi hierarchy expressed a desire to hang von Galen, more subtle forms of retribution were decided upon in order not to alienate public opinion in time of war, and not to make a martyr of him. Yet, as a result of von Galen's daring outspokenness, the euthanasia program was essentially halted.[96]

Christoph Probst was appalled and disgusted when he heard about *Aktion T4*. He expressed the reasons for his outrage to his sister Angelika: "It is not given to any human being, in any circumstance, to make judgments that are reserved to God alone. No one can know what goes on in the soul of a mentally afflicted person. No one can know what secret inner ripening can come from suffering and sorrow. Every individual's life is priceless. We are all dear to God."[97]

A copy of one of von Galen's stirring sermons appeared one day in the Scholl mailbox from an anonymous sender. The fact that someone had had the courage to speak out against the perpetration of inhumanity and had called people to passive resistance was both astonishing and encouraging. Hans, who happened to be home in Ulm at the time, read the sermon and said: "Finally someone has the courage to speak!" and then added, "One ought to have a duplicating machine."[98]

The boldness of Bishop von Galen's sermons and their clandestine manner of dissemination inspired Hans and Alexander. At about this time, in conversation with Lilo Ramdohr, Alexander made mysterious references to "secret postal delivery."[99] It appears that Hans and Alexander were beginning to consider expressing their resistance in concrete ways that went beyond expressions of disapproval in conversations within a small circle of trusted friends. But this was still 1941. It would be a year before the White Rose began to act in earnest.

The souls of Alexander and his friends were aching in distress at the malignant state of their country. Yet they were also young—and glad of it. At times they enjoyed life with childish abandon.[100] They went on hikes, lay in the tall summer grass and watched the clouds, attended concerts of classical music, drank tea and wine, sang together, fell in and out of love. "They met and talked and laughed in favored cafes and restaurants," writes Hanser of the young people.

> Though they were never free of the sense of a menace closing in, … their relish for life and for each other was never wholly extinguished. The pleasure they took in each other's company was one of the most sustaining and replenishing elements in their lives. They never felt so secure, stimulated, and alive as when they were together. Comradeship was not only a sustaining bond among them, but it represented something pure, shining and certain in a world where almost nothing else was left untainted and uncorrupted.[101]

They were even able to take the privations of wartime life with a sense of humor. Alexander and Hans had each long been in need of a new bicycle, but such a wish was unattainable at the time. So they exchanged bikes, and in this way each had a "new," though rather rusty, one.

But the darkness around them grew ever blacker. The population suffered from escalating shortages of food and basic necessities, which made everyday life burdensome and depressing. At the same time, informers proliferated, clouding even the most innocent and incidental human interaction with doubt and suspicion. A professor at the University of Munich named Fritz-Joachim von Rintelen, who had suffused his lectures on ancient Greek thought with criticism of the regime—"using the Greek past to score points against the Nazi present"[102]—abruptly ceased to show up for lectures without any explanation from the university authorities.

The "Final Solution to the Jewish Question," the decision by Hitler's regime to completely destroy the Jewish people, was put into effect in the summer of 1941. *Kristallnacht*, back in 1938, had already unleashed Nazi savagery against Jews in Germany, covering the streets of its cities with broken glass from the smashed windows of Jewish-owned stores and homes. Synagogues had been burned, thousands of Jews had been arrested and incarcerated.

Now, three years later, the systematic annihilation of Jews in the East began. SS firing squads conducted mass executions with unprecedented brutality and deadly efficiency. Slavs in the occupied territories suffered a similar fate,[103] as both Jews and Slavs were regarded as *Untermenschen* (inferior beings) and therefore subject to liquidation or exploitation.

Naturally, German newspapers did not report such things. However, a Munich architect named Manfred Eickemeyer, who spent much time traveling about the occupied East while working on construction ventures there, had witnessed many atrocities. He told his young friends, Hans and Alexander,[104] about the mass executions, the herding of people into concentration camps to be used as slave labor, the forcing of young women into

SS bordellos. Alexander had already confided to Nikolai Hamazaspian his distress at seeing the mistreatment of Jews, who were not allowed to ride buses and had to wear the yellow Star of David. But to Alexander, the massive pogroms conducted by the Nazis in the German-occupied East were inhuman to a fiendish degree.[105] This systematic barbarity depressed him—such a breakdown of societal norms seemed to herald the demise of all humankind.[106] With this new development, the war had taken on apocalyptic dimensions.

Then, in June 1941, Hitler declared war on Russia. Under the guise of eradicating Communism, he intended to make himself master of the boundless expanses of the East, and subsequently to create a new world order under the dominion of the German Reich. Hitler's war on the "racially inferior" Slavs and Jews of Eastern Europe was to be a war of annihilation. In his so-called "Commissar Order," he told his generals: "This struggle is one of ideologies and racial differences and will have to be conducted with unprecedented, unmerciful, and unrelenting harshness."[107]

For Alexander, the war on Russia was personally devastating. He was both Russian and German by heritage, and now the two countries had embarked on a course of mutual enmity and bloodshed. This put him—a man in a German uniform—in a quandary. As he would state in his interrogation by the Gestapo: "Because I am part German, that part of me is being thoroughly annihilated by the current war." He is concerned about Germany, and would like to "protect the German people from the dangers of a major conquest and from the outbreak of additional conflicts." And at the same time, "I readily avow my love for Russia. . . . My mother was Russian, I was born there, and I cannot do otherwise but care about this country. . . . However, I do not identify Russia with Bolshevism. On the contrary, I am a declared enemy of Bolshevism."[108]

Alexander's love of Russia had communicated itself to his friends. From their reading and discussion of Russian classics—Pushkin, Lermontov, Turgenev, Goncharov, and especially Dostoevsky—they had developed an active interest in Russian culture. The Probst siblings, Christoph and Angelika, even started learning the Russian language. Hans added a Russian touch to his daily life by acquiring a Russian samovar for making tea. And thus Alexander's friends, who refused to accept the Nazi view of Russia as a nation of ignorant, uncivilized *Untermenschen*, shared his dismay at the fact that Germany had turned against Russia.

Moreover, and perhaps more importantly, the prospect of war on two fronts boded more misery and suffering for Germans and their adversaries alike. It was becoming ever clearer to the White Rose circle that Hitler had "exceeded all measure, that he had become a maniacal criminal who thought nothing of depriving both his own people and other nations of their external and inner freedoms, and that he was prepared to sacrifice the German people."[109]

In May 1942, the city of Cologne was almost entirely demolished by Allied bombs. In late October, the bombs started falling on Munich, and air raid shelters had to be constructed. Finally, at an evening gathering, someone said: "Isn't it preposterous that we sit in our rooms and study how to heal mankind, when, on the outside, the state every day sends countless young people to their deaths? What in the world are we waiting for? Until one day the war is over, and all nations point to us and say that we accepted this government without resisting?"[110]

CHAPTER 7

Bringing the Truth to Light

The time for action had come. Sometime in the spring of 1942, perhaps even before Sophie arrived in Munich, Alexander and Hans had come to a mutual understanding that they had to advance from their state of inner resistance to an active opposition to the Nazi regime.

Their aim was to make people aware that Hitler did not have the support of the entire German population; to reach out to others who were in opposition to the regime and thereby strengthen them; and to convince the undecided to overcome their hesitation and join the ranks of opposition. In this way, they hoped to foster popular resistance to the National Socialist regime within Germany and, if possible, to shorten the war. The latter, Alexander would state in his interrogation, they saw as the best possible solution for both Germany and Russia.[111]

Their method was to write and disseminate leaflets by which they sought to stir up their apathetic countrymen. Alluding both to current events and to timeless but endangered moral values, the authors penned leaflets that were "an exhortation to reflection, to decision-making, to passive resistance, to sabotage, to non-compliance."[112] Such a course of action was fraught with danger, but that was a risk both Hans and Alexander were willing to take.

Four leaflets were written by Alexander and Hans in the space of several weeks sometime between mid-June and mid-July 1942. Alexander borrowed a typewriter from a friend; a second-hand duplicating machine was purchased, together with paper, envelopes, and stamps. Soon people all over Munich and its environs were receiving seditious leaflets in the mail. Recipients of the leaflets (whose addresses the students got from phone books and city directories) were mostly people of the educated classes—writers, academics, doctors, and owners of bookstores; however, pub keepers and restaurant owners also received leaflets. Some leaflets appeared in the university.

The first leaflet was headed "Leaflets of the White Rose." The reason why Alexander and Hans chose the name "White Rose" for the heading is an enigma. In his interrogation, Hans named a poem by the nineteenth-century Romantic poet Clemens Brentano, in which a character named Rosablanka appears, as the origin of the designation, while also stating that the name was chosen at random. During her interrogation, Sophie makes mention of the white rose being a symbol used by exiled aristocracy during the French Revolution. Lilo Ramdohr maintains that it came from a friend's letter that she shared with Alexander, in which a white rose was mentioned as a symbol of death, love, and youth. Another friend had told Alexander that white roses were the favorite flowers of the last Russian empress, Alexandra, to which he replied, "Yes! The white rose is a symbol of beauty and purity."[113] Nikolai Hamazaspian suggests that the source of the name was Dostoyevsky's legend of the Grand Inquisitor, in which Christ resurrects a young girl who is holding a bouquet of white roses—an image of purity and eternal life.

The leaflet opened with the words: "Nothing is more unworthy of a civilized nation than to allow itself, without resistance, to be governed by an irresponsible ruling clique that is motivated by the darkest instinct." Every honest German, the leaflet asserts, is ashamed of his current government. "Who among us has any conception of the dimensions of shame that will befall us and our children when one day the veil has fallen from our eyes and the most horrible of crimes—crimes that infinitely outdistance every human measure—reach the light of day?" It is man's free will that raises him above all other God's creatures. Instead of abandoning this free will and becoming a spiritless and cowardly mass, the German people must take decisive action, exhort the authors of the leaflet. One should not wait for the next person to make a start. "Every individual, conscious of his responsibility as a member of Christian and Western civilization must … work against the scourges of mankind, against fascism and any similar form of the absolute state. Offer passive resistance—*resistance*—wherever you may be, forestall the spread of this atheistic war machine before it is too late."[114] At the bottom of the leaflet was written the following: "Please make as many copies of this leaflet as you can and distribute them."

Christoph Probst knew of the leaflets, approved of them as a way to "gamble our 'No' against this power which has arrogantly placed itself above the essential human values,"[115] and was consulted in the matter of their writing. Alexander and Hans, however, did not want to involve him directly in the perils of disseminating the leaflets, as he was a family man, and they ardently wished to shield him from any possible repercussions.

Initially, Sophie also was not included in the work of the two. But once she found out, she joined wholeheartedly in reproducing the texts on the mimeograph machine, acquiring paper and stamps, addressing envelopes, and mailing and distributing the leaflets. A second leaflet soon followed. It spoke of the massacre of Jews and the outrages inflicted on the Poles—the first time these had ever been mentioned in print. Citing the fact that, "since the conquest of Poland, *three hundred thousand* Jews have been murdered in that country in a bestial manner," the authors of the leaflet decried this as "the most frightful crime against human dignity, a crime that has no counterpart in human history." The wholesale annihilation of Polish aristocratic youth was similarly bewailed and condemned:

> Why do the German people behave so apathetically in the face of all these abominable crimes, crimes so unworthy of the human race? ... Through his apathy [the German] allows evil men to act as they do ... Each man is guilty, guilty, guilty! ... Up until the outbreak of the war the larger part of the German people was blinded; the Nazis did not show themselves in their true aspect. But now that we have recognized them for what they are, it must be the sole and first duty, the holiest duty of every German, to destroy these beasts.

If any good comes of Germany's catastrophe, "it will only be by virtue of the fact that we are cleansed by suffering; that in the midst of deepest night we yearn for the light, summon up our strength, and finally rise up to shake off the yoke which weighs on our world."

The third leaflet, which followed in close succession, proclaimed that "our present 'state' is the dictatorship of evil." Addressing the reader directly, the authors of the leaflet insisted: "It is your *moral duty* to eliminate the system." But, the authors stated, it is not possible to effectively oppose "this offspring of Hell" through solitary withdrawal. Only collective passive resistance can bring "this monster of a state to an end." The leaflet went on to suggest methods of resistance: sabotage in armament plants, war industries, and every scientific or intellectual field that would aid in continuing the war; sabotage of newspapers and publications that help to disseminate "the brown lie"; sabotage at all gatherings, rallies, and public ceremonies that promote National Socialism. "Do not give a penny to public drives," advocated the leaflet. "Do not contribute to the collections of scrap metal, textiles and the like." In conclusion, the leaflet quoted Aristotle's *Politics*: "A tyrant is inclined to engage in constant warfare in order to occupy and distract his subjects."

The fourth leaflet recognized the demonic aspects of National Socialism and Hitler himself: "Every word that comes from Hitler's mouth is a lie. When he says peace, he means war, and when he blasphemously uses the name of the Almighty, he means the power of evil, the fallen angel, Satan. His mouth is the foul-smelling pit of Hell, and his power is at bottom accursed." The authors of the leaflet insisted that in conducting a struggle against the National Socialist terrorist state, the true nature of this struggle must be clearly understood: "[It is] a struggle against the devil, against the servants of the Antichrist. . . . Without the true God, [man] is defenseless against the principle of evil."

What was needed, then, was for religion to reawaken Europe. But for this reawakening to take place, along with a "renewal from within of the severely wounded German spirit," it had to be preceded by a "clear recognition of all the guilt with which the German people have burdened themselves." The leaflet ended with the words: "We will not be silent. We are your bad conscience. The White Rose will not leave you in peace!"

CHAPTER 8

Birch Trees and Bloodshed

For a time, however, no further leaflets appeared. The authors had been called to the Russian front with the Second Student-Military Company. Alexander, Hans, Willi Graf and two more close friends, Jürgen Wittenstein[116] and Hubert Furtwängler,[117] departed for Russia on July 23, 1942.[118] Three days later, their train arrived in Warsaw. The Nazi-inflicted atrocities that had been mentioned in the White Rose leaflets—the "crimes that infinitely outdistance every human measure"[119]—were about to become a reality for them. What the young men saw as they walked about the city shook them deeply: rubble and devastation, the wretchedness of the Jewish ghetto behind walls and barbed-wire fences, and starving children lying on sidewalks and begging for food. "Misery stares us in the face," wrote Willi in his diary.[120]

Sickened by what they saw, they were only too glad to leave.

As the train made its way into Russia and the zone of recent conflict, they were greeted by views of beautiful, limitless landscapes amid which stood cities in ruins. When they disembarked at one of the cities, all they encountered was "filth, misery, and German marching music," recorded Willi.[121] At last, they reached their final destination, Gzhatsk, about sixty miles west of Moscow. The student medics were assigned to work as physician's assistants at a casualty clearing station.

"We traveled for a total of twelve days," wrote Alexander in his first letter home from Russia. "The front lies about ten kilometers from here. Gzhatsk itself is almost entirely destroyed and the Russians continue to shell it, now by day, now by night. However," continued Alexander, attempting to assuage his family's fears for his safety, "our camp is in the forest and perfectly safe."[122] Hans, writing home to his family, was more forthright in depicting the situation. "The partisans are incredibly active," he reported. "They pose a genuine threat to our supply lines. In this area, they blew up forty-eight trains in a single week. . . . And paratroops land behind our lines, day after day and night after night."[123]

For Alexander this was a homecoming—it was the first time he had seen Russia as an adult. Through him, Hans and Willi were able to feel a bond with Russia and its inhabitants. They rambled about together in the

Russian countryside. Alexander felt at one with Russian nature, which he had come to love from childhood through his father's tales about "the steppe and the wide expanses which will always be there, the forests and the mountains over which Man is not lord."[124] In the birch tree, so prevalent in Russia, he finds metaphorical meaning. There, in the Russian land, "far, far away, where heaven and earth meet, at the edge of a vast and endless plain, it stands alone and points towards heaven. O you lonely birch tree, the perpetual wind of the steppes caresses, dishevels, breaks you; you are its eternal plaything. And isn't the Russian man like you? ... Is he not also the plaything of Life?"[125]

Although "fraternizing with the enemy" put them at risk with their superiors, in their free time the young medics ate, talked, sang, and danced with the local inhabitants. "Despite their poverty, the people here are extraordinarily hospitable," reported Alexander. "As soon as you walk in the door, the samovar and absolutely everything that is to be found in the house is put on the table. . . . I have not encountered anything other than kindness here."[126] Willi offered a further glimpse of these meetings with the local Russians: "We sit with peasants and sing together and they sing wonderful old songs. You forget for a whole moment all the sadness and the horror that is happening around you. It's interesting that the simplest people: peasants, fishermen, craftsmen, know Dostoevsky and are involved in what he writes—not superficially but in the deepest sense."[127] Alexander often called at the home of the local village priest and spent long days fishing with a grizzled old fisherman.[128] In speaking with the Russians—peasants, workers, and intelligentsia—Alexander came to the conclusion that "there is nothing in the world that they despise more than Bolshevism. And, most important, even if the war ends unfavorably for Germany, Bolshevism will never return to Russia. It has been done away with once and for all; the Russian people hate it too much."[129]

Thousands of Orthodox churches that had been closed by the Bolsheviks were now reopened in Russian territory under German occupation. These immediately filled with believers, who had not lost their faith during the intervening twenty years, initiating what has been called a "spiritual rebirth." Hans, who attended Orthodox services with Alexander while in Russia, was moved to write of one such service: "One could sense the stirring, the outpouring of souls unfolding after a long and terrible silence, souls that had at last found their way back to their true home. I could have wept for joy. . . . The veil of cloud is rent asunder, as it were, by the sunlight of a new religious awakening."[130] These experiences in Russia lead Alexander to entertain thoughts of staying on there rather than returning to Germany.

But there was another world that the friends inhabited—that of war, which, seen first-hand, was ugly and senseless. "I have no music in me anymore," wrote

Hans. "All I hear all day and night are groans of men in pain."[131] One day, Hans and Alexander came upon the dismembered, decomposing corpse of a Russian soldier lying unburied in a field where a battle had occurred. They dug a grave in which they placed the remains. "We ended by nailing a Russian cross together and sticking it in the ground at the head. Now his soul is at rest," wrote Hans in his diary.[132]

In the beginning of September, Alexander suddenly fell ill with diphtheria. For several weeks he remained bedridden. Not wanting to worry his family, he was reluctant to inform them of his condition. At the beginning of October, when he was already on the mend, Alexander had Hans write a postcard on his behalf, telling his parents that he had been in bed for the past ten days with tonsillitis. "But you shouldn't worry at all," he said, "because the fever and sore throat have subsided."[133] A week later he wrote a short note himself, parenthetically admitting what illness he had actually been suffering from. "I am fully recovered from my illness (diphtheria), am well-fed and healthy, so you have no cause for concern."[134]

In late October, after more than three months at the front, Alexander, Hans, and Willi were recalled together with their student company to Germany. They were reluctant to leave Russia. "It will be very difficult for me to part with all my acquaintances here," wrote Alexander to his parents, "but I hope it won't be for long."[135] And Willi noted in his diary: "I'm leaving Russia with a heavy heart."[136] Certain troubling aspects of the war persistently intruded on them. As they wended their way home by train, they continued to witness Nazi German brutality, which they attempted to counteract several times. In one such incident, while stopped at the Polish border, they saw German guards abusing a group of emaciated Russian prisoners of war. Not able to contain their pity, Alexander, Hans, and Willi attempted to mitigate the prisoners' plight by offering them their army-issue cigarettes. When the guards broke out in violent curses, an altercation ensued that could have escalated, had the train not started moving, forcing the threesome to jump back on.

They mulled over and discussed what their course of action would be once they got back to Munich. While in Russia, Hans had received news of his father's arrest for calling Hitler "God's scourge on mankind."[137] He was returning from Russia with an even firmer conviction of the necessity to continue his resistance work. Although Alexander had been inclined to remain in Russia, he nevertheless felt duty-bound to return to Germany to continue the work on which he and Hans had embarked. What the student-medics had seen at the front—the unimaginable scale of human suffering, the senseless cruelty, bloodshed, and loss of life—had reinforced their conviction that the regime that they had assailed in their first four leaflets must be defied even more energetically. This time, they would redouble their efforts—they would endeavor to broaden their contacts, to build a network of like-minded people. It was imperative to thwart this regime—and its obsession for annihilating anything that stood in its way—at all costs, to put a stop to the war that pointlessly carried away hundreds of lives every day. Moreover, didn't the fact that they had gotten away with distributing their leaflets with no reprisal indicate that the Third Reich was not unassailable?[138]

CHAPTER 9

Another Alexander

The student-medics arrived in Munich on November 6, 1942.

The mood in Germany was grim, morale was low. There were air raids and strict rationing of food and other wartime scarcities.[139] In the words of Lilo Ramdohr, "the specters of horror multiplied like vermin, gnawing away at the endurance of every person, and lodging ever deeper into the substance of one's life-sustaining forces, which clearly have their limits. Everyone had the loss of friends and relatives to mourn, and all of us found ourselves in immediate mortal danger."[140] It looked like invasion might be expected from the West, and the German army was experiencing setbacks in northern Africa and in the East. The young men had seen for themselves the terrible condition of the German troops in Russia, and to them it was obvious that Germany was going to lose the war.

The Russian Orthodox parish of St Nicholas in Munich where Alexander and Nyanya attended services was experiencing wartime privations. The church building could be heated only occasionally. The number of people attending services had increased dramatically with the influx of Russian émigrés from occupied France and Belgium, and with the arrival of the *Ostarbeiter* (Eastern workers) who had been brought from the Slavic countries to perform forced labor in Germany.[141] The parish found that it could not adequately provide the newcomers with icons and crosses. The rationing of paper made it difficult to publish the spiritual literature urgently needed to educate the new arrivals from the East, those who had had no access to spiritual literature under the Communist rule of their homeland. Even candles came to be in short supply and had to be cut in half. In December 1942, Metropolitan Serafim (Lade), head of the German diocese, wrote from Berlin that the diocesan administration was no longer able to provide the parish with flour for prosphora[142] or wine for communion and suggested that an appeal be made to the parishioners for donations of flour from their own rations.

There was, however, good news along with the bad. For many years, because of a scarcity of priests, the parish of St Nicholas had not been able to have services with any regularity.[143] The situation improved somewhat in

1937 when Fr Alexander (Lovchii) was designated by the Russian Church Outside of Russia as supply priest for a number of parishes in Bavaria, including Munich. In August 1942, he was assigned as full-time rector of St Nicholas.[144] At last the parish was able to have regular services on weekends and feast days.[145]

Every Sunday, Fr Alexander would address his congregation in sermons that sought to catechize them, exhort them to live a truly Christian life, and support them in the burdens of émigré wartime existence. These sermons were printed in a two-page leaflet entitled *Voskresnyi Listok* (Sunday Bulletin), which also included announcements and was handed out to parishioners.

Aside from explaining timeless doctrinal truths and the way of salvation, Fr Alexander would touch on themes that had contemporary significance.[146] Russia—and with it the Russian Orthodox Church Outside of Russia—had embarked on a course of untold suffering and oppression ever since the Russian Revolution. Could the Russian émigrés help Russia, even though they were beyond its borders? Yes, "we must preserve the legacy of spiritual enlightenment that we have received from our fathers and transmit it to the younger generations that are growing up both outside of Russia and, later, within Russia."[147]

Although his flock had escaped the persecution and suppression of Christianity in Russia by the godless, spiritual danger was lurking in the country where they had found shelter. In his sermon of October 26, 1942,

Fr Alexander cautioned against the "crude egotistical instincts and aspirations and false moral concepts which have developed in fallen humankind," giving rise to a "breakdown in all personal, familial, social, national and international relations" that threaten the very existence of mankind.

When a nation strives to subjugate or eradicate others, continued Fr Alexander in the same sermon, and "looks upon other nations as its natural enemies, as a race of beings who have an entirely different nature," this has nothing in common with Christianity. Christianity, he said, teaches not racial superiority but the brotherhood of man. In the Christian view, which sees "all men as sons of one God-Father, nations are called not to stifle others or eliminate them from the path of history," but to learn from one another, each "seeking to adopt from others the best of what they have developed, and sharing the finest fruits of their own development." On a more personal level, the concept of love for one's neighbor—which, Fr Alexander noted, has been held in respect throughout history even by non-Christian civilizations—means "love for those who especially need love: compassion for the weak, the defenseless, the needy, the suffering." In this way, the Christian concept of love, as embodied in the relations between individuals and nations, ensures the continued existence of mankind.[148]

Speaking on November 22, Fr Alexander stressed the immutability of Christian doctrine, and the need to witness to it even in the face of possible unpleasantness, persecution, or even death. "All evil derives from the fact that some people, due to their own kindness, do not denounce those who, by their commands and words sow doubt into the hearts and minds of others and thereby give them the opportunity for subsequent evildoing."[149]

In December, when the bleakness of winter reflected the grim desolation of life in wartime Nazi Germany, Fr Alexander summed up the prevailing mood with these words: "As a result of the confusion, strife, treachery and killings all around, people have fallen into fear and despair, and almost everyone has lost hope in the security of their lives and property."[150] Throughout these dismal months, the pastor called his flock not to feel forsaken by God, but rather to attain a deeper understanding of their hardships and misfortunes. Although sufferings accompany all people throughout their entire lives, from birth to death, they are transitory; their reward is as eternal as God himself.[151] The highest level of a Christian's attitude toward suffering, in Fr Alexander's understanding, is the ability to come to love it, after which sorrow is transformed into joy—the joy of imitating Christ in His sufferings. "Whoever suffers for a just cause ... may be happy, having done so. Suffering tempers the character and forms real people."[152] As things went from bad to worse, Fr Alexander reminded his flock that, even while undergoing suffering, one can obtain joy and comfort from observing the beauties of nature, from delighting in all that is noble and glorious, from helping others, and above all from prayer.[153]

Alexander Schmorell was among those attending services at the parish of St Nicholas and listening to the weekly sermons that winter (indeed, a friend recalled that Alexander never missed a service).[154] In a letter to a young woman he had met in Russia, Alexander described his impressions of life in the parish: "Recently 1,700 Russians have been sent here—so now we've got lots of Russians here. . . . Our church is always filled to overflowing—that's where everyone sees each other; our priest is a real treasure—such a good man. His primary concern is to help the Russians, to comfort them. The choristers are also good, they sing splendidly."[155] Did Fr Alexander's sermons—the boldness of their thinly veiled criticism of the anti-Christian and racist ideology of the Third Reich, his call to stand up for truth, his explanation of suffering—exert an influence on Alexander? Did the two discuss these matters in private? That belongs to the realm of conjecture, yet it seems possible that Fr Alexander's statements—so congruent with the White Rose stance—may have, at the very least, confirmed Alexander in his thoughts and in the moral rightness of his actions, and strengthened his resolve. For earlier in this same letter, Alexander, after expressing his homesickness for Russia and hopes for returning there soon, said: "But I *must* nevertheless remain in Germany." He and his friends were determined—and felt a moral obligation—to carry on their resistance activities. It is this commitment that "gives me a moral right to remain here [in Germany],"[156] wrote Alexander to another Russian friend, without divulging what the commitment was.

CHAPTER 10

We Will Not Be Silent

Resuming the life they had led before their assignment to Russia—studying, attending concerts, and participating in evenings of reading and discussion—the students also set about planning the next phase of their resistance work. They discussed the desirability of forming a broad anti-Nazi front, of establishing contact with other resisters in Germany. While their first four leaflets had been aimed at well-educated readers, this time they would reach out to a wider audience, to the average man in the street. Leaflets would have to be produced in larger quantities. This would necessitate a serious financial outlay. Hans and Alexander solicited the aid of Eugen Grimminger, a friend of the Scholl parents with anti-Nazi leanings, who contributed well over 1,500 Reichsmarks.[157]

Soon Alexander and Hans had drafted a new leaflet—the fifth. This time the leaflet did not bear the name of the White Rose, but proclaimed itself to be a "Leaflet of the Resistance Movement in Germany: A Call to All Germans." In its first paragraph, the leaflet asserted:

> It has become a mathematical certainty that Hitler is leading the German people into the abyss. *Hitler cannot win the war; he can only prolong it.* The guilt of Hitler and his minions exceeds all bounds. Retribution comes closer and closer. But what are the German people doing? They will not see and will not listen. Blindly they follow their seducers into ruin.

It is imperative to disassociate oneself from "National Socialist gangsterism" without delay, exhorts the leaflet. "Prove by your deeds that you think otherwise. . . . Cast off the cloak of indifference you have wrapped around you! Decide *before it is too late*!" A new war of liberation is about to begin, and "the better part of the nation will fight on our side." A New Europe is about to emerge— one that is based on freedom of speech, freedom of religion, and the protection of individual citizens from the arbitrary will of violent criminal regimes. The leaflet closes with a final appeal: "Support the resistance. Distribute the leaflets!"

Whereas the first four leaflets had been reproduced in quantities of several hundred, this time there were thousands. Copies were made, one by one, night after night, on a hand-cranked duplicating machine, with the students taking turns at this arduous and tiring task. Then there was the work of addressing hundreds upon hundreds of envelopes with addresses that had been gleaned from phone books. "Subversion as practiced by the Munich students," observes Hanser, "demanded more than idealism, courage, and a sense of outrage. It also demanded the utmost in patience, endurance, and sheer drudgery."[158]

To disseminate the leaflets more widely, and to give the impression of a large network while diverting suspicion from Munich, the students would travel by train, with the leaflets in their luggage, and mail them in various cities to yet another city. Hans posted 150 leaflets from Salzburg. Alexander traveled with 1,400 leaflets to Linz, Vienna, and Frankfurt. Leaflets appeared in Stuttgart, Ulm, and Augsburg.

Sophie worked tirelessly. She posted leaflets in three cities. To aid in the dissemination of the leaflets, she enlisted the help of two friends from Ulm, the siblings Hans and Susanne Hirzel, who were still in high school. In turn, Hans Hirzel drafted some of his friends for the cause.

Traute Lafrenz brought copies of two leaflets to Hamburg. There they were received with enthusiasm by dissident students and intellectuals who reproduced and disseminated them. (Later, these people would become known as the "Hamburg Branch of the White

Rose.") Willi Graf embarked on visits to several cities (Bonn, Saarbrücken, Freiburg, and Cologne), bearing not only leaflets but also a duplicating machine in his large suitcase, and attempting to win support for the cause of resistance at the universities. Reactions to his proposals were varied, but in Saarbrücken, an old friend of Willi's named Willi Bollinger took the duplicating machine and some leaflets to reproduce and disseminate. Having acquired some forging skills, Bollinger in turn provided Willi Graf with forged military passes, leave papers, and army railroad tickets for future use by members of the White Rose.

Even such seemingly simple and innocuous things as the acquisition of stamps, paper, and envelopes were difficult and fraught with danger. Paper goods were in short supply in wartime, and thus Sophie and Traute had to acquire them in small quantities at various stores. Additionally, one must try not to arouse suspicion—what could a student possibly want with hundreds of stamps and envelopes?

Traveling by train to mail the leaflets in other cities posed great risks and difficulties. The young people always undertook these trips alone. Boarding the train in one compartment, they would stow the suitcase holding the incriminating leaflets there, then take a seat in another compartment to be as far away as possible if the leaflets were found. After passing through various checks (the Gestapo and military police were searching for deserters, fugitives, and food smugglers), the courier would arrive at a planned destination and deposit the leaflets in various mailboxes around the city.

When their supply of envelopes ran out, Willi, Alexander, and Hans sallied forth at night to distribute more than two thousand leaflets throughout Munich, depositing them in courtyards and entryways and on sidewalks. Sophie even risked distributing by day a small quantity of leaflets, which she placed in Munich telephone booths and on parked cars. The authorities became decidedly uneasy. "The appearance of this relatively large number of leaflets in the 'Capital of the [Nazi] Movement' had understandably caused alarm and consternation all the way to the highest levels," divulged Gestapo interrogator Robert Mohr in an interview many years later.[159]

In undertaking their activities of resistance, the students were knowingly placing themselves in great peril. When Lilo Ramdohr cautioned Alexander about the possible consequences of his resistance work, he answered: "There's no going back now … I will not leave Hans in the lurch. He is my friend."[160] Later on, Alexander told the Gestapo:

> We fully realized that the publication of treasonous flyers constituted an action against the National Socialist regime, which would lead to the heaviest penalties should we be found out. Therefore, what I did, I did not do unwittingly, but rather

I counted on the possibility of losing my life should I be found out. I simply disregarded all of that, because my inner obligation to act against the National Socialist regime prevailed.[161]

Sophie echoed this sentiment when she said, "There are so many people dying *for* this regime; it is high time that someone died *opposing* it."[162]

CHAPTER 11

In the Midst of Deepest Night

Theirs was a lonely burden. It wasn't only the authorities whose detection the students were avoiding. They could not even reveal their activities to their families and closest friends, for fear of compromising them. (Knowledge of subversive activities was construed by the Nazi state as tantamount to active participation and punishable just as severely.) Thus they were deprived of the emotional support of those whom they loved and esteemed most, and were forced to live double lives, attending lectures and fulfilling their hospital duties by day and cranking out leaflets by night.

An incident at the University of Munich gave rise to the hope that other students would support the work of resistance. On January 13, 1943, the university celebrated the 470th anniversary of its founding. Students and faculty were ordered to attend a gathering that was to be addressed by a prominent Nazi official named Giesler. In keeping with their policy of boycotting Nazi rallies and assemblies, the White Rose students were absent, but some of their friends had come out of curiosity. Giesler addressed the students with a diatribe against those who were using their studies to avoid their war duties either at the front or in war plants. The female students, said Giesler, were wasting their time in intellectual pursuits and would be better off in their "natural place," at home, giving birth to children annually as a contribution to Fatherland and Führer. He followed this up with an exceedingly crude remark, which set off an outburst of protest that spilled out into the streets of Munich, with students marching, singing, and chanting in unison. They were dispersed by the police. A state of emergency was declared in Munich, but the incident was hushed up in the press. Although the protest was short-lived, Hans and Alexander heard the news with joy. The protest seemed to indicate that at last things were taking a turn for what they had hoped. And perhaps their own leaflets had played a role in stirring the students to exhibit some semblance of resistance.

On February 3, 1943, the German people were staggered by news of a new calamity. On that day, German radio interrupted its regular programming with a special announcement. The Battle of Stalingrad had come to an end. After six months of devastating and desperate fighting—Hitler had ordered that retreat or surrender was out of the question, and that German troops should fight to the last man—what was left of the mighty German Sixth Army had capitulated. The loss of more than three hundred thousand men at Stalingrad was the worst military disaster in German history and a major turning point in the war.

The reaction of the German people was one of stunned disbelief and great sorrow. The Nazi regime responded to the Stalingrad fiasco by intensifying its campaign of intimidation and terror, sentencing its subjects to death for the slightest infraction.[163]

The southern German cities were experiencing an influx of refugees from the cities in the north, which had been bombed into oblivion by the Allies. Shortage, hunger, alarm, despair, and dread were everywhere. It looked like German society was disintegrating.

It was time for another leaflet. A new collaborator put his pen to paper—a professor named Kurt Huber who had been invited to join the circle of student resisters sometime in 1942. Professor Huber lectured on philosophy, probing what great minds had said about the order of the cosmos and about divine justice in its relation to evil. Students, seeing their world completely engulfed by abomination, packed Huber's lecture hall and listened with great interest, appreciative of his eloquence and subtle insights, which were sometimes accompanied by subversive innuendoes. Huber had been befriended by the White Rose students and became one of their mentors.

Now, prompted by the tragedy of Stalingrad and by the disturbance among the student body caused by Giesler's offensive speech at the university's anniversary, the professor authored the sixth and final leaflet. His stated purpose: "to arouse the student community to a moral evaluation of the existing evils in our political life."[164]

Speaking in the name of German youth, it was addressed "To Fellow Students" and began with the words: "Shaken and broken, our people behold the loss of our men at Stalingrad. Three hundred and thirty thousand German men have been senselessly and irresponsibly driven to death and destruction by the brilliant strategy of that World War I corporal. Führer, we thank you!"

Enumerating the ills of the Nazi regime that had especially affected the youth of Germany, the leaflet called for students to rally and resist: "Freedom and honor! For ten long years, Hitler and his comrades have manhandled, twisted and debased these two splendid words to the point of nausea." These ten years, Huber wrote, had seen the destruction of all material and intellectual freedoms and of the moral fiber of the German people by a ruling class that consists of godless, impudent, and conscienceless exploiters and executioners.

The leaflet thanked the students who reacted so bravely to Giesler's "besmirching of the honor" of the women students for setting a brilliant example. Their protest was "the beginning of the struggle for our free self-determination." And now, Huber continued, "the day of reckoning has come—the reckoning of German youth with the most abominable tyrant our people have ever been forced to endure. . . . The name of Germany will remain forever stained with shame if German youth do not finally rise up. The German people look to us! … The dead of Stalingrad beseech us!"

Once again, the friends busied themselves with cranking out hundreds upon hundreds of leaflets, addressing envelopes, affixing stamps. When they ran out of envelopes, they folded the leaflets and addressed them on the outside. Addresses were copied out of a student directory that Professor Huber had given them. Hans, Willi, and Alexander mailed more than one thousand leaflets at night from various locations throughout Munich.

Throughout this winter, Alexander's peace seems to have left him. In early December, he divulged to a friend: "Disquiet (*Unruhe*), dreadful disquiet is the prevailing characteristic of my life here. . . . No calm minute of respite is granted to me. The source of this disquiet—who knows? Perhaps my character, perhaps a longing for my homeland, perhaps both."[165] Alexander shut himself up in his room for hours on end, immersing himself in sculpting in the hopes that his creative work would bring him tranquility. "Only work … (by work I mean only sculpting) … is my peace," he wrote on December 23.[166] Yet the sensation of disquiet continued to pursue him doggedly. In January, he was still bewailing the fact that "bleakness and sadness" were his "constant companions."[167]

Could his disquiet have been caused by the unrelenting tension of Alexander's resistance work or even a presentiment of doom? Lilo Ramdohr wrote of this period: "Alex almost certainly had forebodings inasmuch, as at this time all the friends, especially Hans Scholl, were beset by a pressing disquiet."[168] This, however, did not prevent them from carrying on their self-imposed burden of chipping away at the Nazi stranglehold on their country.

During the night of February 3, Alexander, Hans, and Willi embarked on a new perilous nocturnal adventure. Using stencils that Alexander had prepared and some tar paint, the young men ventured out in the dead of night to paint graffiti on the walls of the busiest parts of the city. Two would paint, while the third stood watch. On the morning after this foray, the citizens of Munich woke up to see the words "Hitler is a mass murderer," "Down with Hitler!" and "Freedom!" conspicuously emblazoned in large letters on apartment houses, public buildings, and monuments, including the *Feldherrnhalle*, a nineteenth-century military monument that had become sacred to the Nazis for its association with Hitler's Beer Hall Putsch. Accompanying some of the slogans were white swastikas crossed out with red paint. Such overt defiance caused a decided stir. Passersby gaped in disbelief at the slogans' audacity. Twice more, on the nights of February 8 and 15, the young men set out to paint their audacious slogans. The authorities deployed Russian women laborers to scrub away the offending words, while they themselves launched an investigation to find the perpetrators of this brazen challenge to the Nazi state.

In their defiant actions against the Nazi state, the group was taking ever greater risks, getting ever more reckless. At the same time, they had received hints that the authorities were on their trail and that they were in danger of being apprehended. Thoughts of fleeing entered their minds but were put aside. It was necessary to catalyze a wave of unrest, to spur dormant resistance—preferably among the university students—into action. Around February 10, Alexander brought Lilo news of new plans. "Something is about to happen at the university," he said. But it hadn't yet been decided among the friends how this "something" was going to take place. Alexander wasn't counting on an auspicious outcome. He talked of making plans for an escape.[169]

CHAPTER 12

We Will Meet in Eternity

During the winter, while listening to radio broadcasts from other countries (a "subversive" act), Alexander and Hans found out that an anti-Nazi resistance group called the Red Orchestra was uncovered in Berlin in the fall of 1942. Aggrieved, like the White Rose, by the Nazis's trampling of Germany's cultural and ethical heritage, the members of the Red Orchestra sought to undermine the faith of the German people in the Nazi regime by writing leaflets recounting its nefarious deeds both at home and abroad. In an attempt to prevent a Nazi victory, they also passed on this information, along with German military secrets, to foreign governments. They aided people who for various reasons were in danger at the hands of the regime and wished to flee Germany. In December 1942, just days before Christmas, fifty members of the

Red Orchestra, many of them women, were tried and executed.[170]

Among the executed was Arvid Harnack, an acquaintance of Lilo Ramdohr. Arvid's brother Falk visited Lilo occasionally in Munich. Alexander asked Lilo to introduce him and Hans to Falk, hoping that the latter could put the White Rose circle in contact with members of the German resistance effort in Berlin. These were members of the Confessing Church, such as Dietrich Bonhoeffer, and people in the military and the government. Some would later be involved with the Valkyrie conspiracy, which unsuccessfully attempted to assassinate Hitler in July 1944.[171] Although this contact would put everyone at risk, Falk agreed. Several meetings took place, during which Hans and Alexander divulged to Falk the details of their leaflet campaign and discussed with him various options for expanded and coordinated resistance efforts. One further meeting with Falk was arranged for February 25, but it never came to pass.

On the morning of Thursday, February 18, Hans and Sophie left for the university, carrying a suitcase filled with leaflets. While classes were in session, they quickly and quietly left piles of leaflets in corridors, on staircases, and on windowsills. Finding that a number of leaflets still remained, they went to the upper floor and placed a pile on the balustrade overlooking the atrium. On a whim, Sophie pushed them off, sending them fluttering down. Unexpectedly, the building custodian happened to be passing through the atrium at that very moment and saw the cascade of paper. Although Hans and Sophie tried to escape by mingling with the students who had started exiting their lecture halls at the end of class, the custodian caught up with them and apprehended them. Soon they were in the custody of the Gestapo.

Hans and Sophie's calm, almost relaxed, demeanor, and plausible explanations nearly convinced the Gestapo that they were not guilty of distributing seditious material. A search of their apartment, however, yielded incriminating evidence: large numbers of stamps and envelopes. The first interrogation, lasting seventeen hours, continued through the night into Friday. Hans and Sophie were interrogated in separate rooms. They were being accused of high treason, which was punishable by death. When it became apparent that, in the face of mounting evidence, denial was no longer feasible, they both confessed.

Even while initially denying any involvement with the leaflets, Sophie had unequivocally affirmed her opposition to National Socialism at the beginning of her interrogation. "I would like to declare that I myself don't want to have anything to do with National Socialism," she stated. Sophie's interrogator attempted to persuade her to renounce her opposition—to state that, in carrying out the work of resistance, she had been blindly and unthinkingly following the example of her brother—and thereby to save her life. Sophie's answer was firm: "If my brother is sentenced to die, you mustn't let them give me a lighter

1. The Schmorell family: Alexander, Hugo, Elisabeth, Natasha, and Erich. Munich, 1930.

2. Alexander Schmorell in conversation with Nyanya.

3. Alexander Schmorell, 1939.

4. Alexander at a university lecture, 1941.

5. Bust of Beethoven, sculpted and photographed by Alexander Schmorell.

6. Saying goodbye at the train station as the student medics leave for Russia, July 23, 1942.
R-L: Alexander Schmorell, Sophie Scholl, unknown, Hans Scholl and Hubert Furtwängler.

7. Sharing a meal in the vicinity of Gzhatsk, Russia, July 1942.
L-R: Hubert Furtwängler, Hans Scholl, Willi Graf and
Alexander Schmorell.

8-9. Gzhatsk, Russia, July 1942. Church services resume under German occupation after
decades of religious persecution by the Communists. Could one of these priests be the one
whom Alexander visited while stationed nearby?

10. Facsimile of the sixth White Rose leaflet.

11. Hans and Sophie were caught distributing leaflets in this hall at the University of Munich.

12. Main building of the University of Munich. This contemporary photo shows the signpost for the semi-circular plaza that now bears the Scholl name.

13. Wanted notice, seeking Alexander, in a Munich newspaper dated February 24, 1943. Headline: "Criminal sought: 1,000 marks reward."

14. The Stadelheim prison guillotine, instrument of Alexander's martyric death.

15. Alexander's nanny, Feodosia Lapschina, many years after his death, in the Church of St Nicholas (at that time located on Salvatorplatz).

16. Father Alexander (Lovchii), Alexander's parish priest who confessed and communed him on the day of execution. Pictured here in 1945, after becoming a bishop, with altar server Paul Urtiew (see note 145 page 187).

17. Russian Orthodox Cathedral of the New Martyrs in Munich, located within walking distance of Stadelheim Prison and Alexander's grave. Alexander's parish acquired the property 50 years after his death.

18. Grave of Alexander Schmorell in the cemetery of Perlacher Forst. His father and stepmother are interred in the same grave.

19. Church procession to Alexander's grave on the eve of his glorification.

20. Prayers at Alexander's grave on the eve of his glorification.

21. At a reception following the glorification, members of the Schmorell family converse with 91-year-old Nikolai Hamazaspian, who in 1943 aided Alexander in his attempted escape from the Gestapo.

22. During the service of glorification, the icon of St Alexander is brought out for the first time for veneration. Immediately behind the icon is Metropolitan Valentin of Orenburg, Russia, the city of Alexander's birth.

23. St Alexander, third from right, depicted among the New Martyrs of Russia in an icon painted before his glorification (thus he is portrayed without a halo). In his hand he holds a scroll inscribed with extracts from his final letters to his family.

24. Scroll detail: "This whole terrible misfortune has been necessary to show me the right way… I am glad, and grateful to God for it, that it has been granted to me to understand this sign from Him … One thing above all I urge upon you: do not forget God!"

25. Icon of St Alexander, painted by Priest Alexij Lemmer for the glorification.

sentence, for I am as guilty as he is." As for being "wrong" in her views about National Socialism, she retorted to the interrogator: "It is not I, but you, who have the wrong worldview. I would do the same all over again."[172]

Casting their nets ever wider, the Gestapo began to bring in and question more and more of the Scholls's collaborators and their relatives. (A facet of Nazi terror was the practice of *Sippenhaft*, or clan arrest, whereby the spouses, parents, siblings, and other relatives of perceived enemies of the state were held to be collectively liable for their kinsman's offense.) As he was being arrested, Hans had tried unsuccessfully to dispose of a sheet of paper he was carrying in his pocket. This was the rough draft of a seventh leaflet, written by Christoph Probst. This leaflet, which was never reproduced or distributed, pleaded: "Will all Germans be sacrificed to the forces of hatred and destruction? Sacrificed to the man who persecuted the Jews, who eradicated half the Poles, and who wanted to annihilate Russia? Sacrificed to the man who took away your freedom, peace, domestic happiness, hope, and joy? ... Hitler and his regime must fall so that Germany may live."

Piecing together the torn-up paper, the Gestapo determined its authorship and soon Christoph, who had known nothing of the Scholls's arrest, joined Hans and Sophie in jail.[173] This was the only time that Sophie lost her composure. To think that Christoph—whom the friends had tried to keep away from any actively compromising

deeds, who was the father of three small children and had a wife still in bed with childbirth fever—would now be called to account for high treason was more than she could bear.

After several days of almost uninterrupted inter-rogations, a trial under the jurisdiction of the People's Court was urgently summoned for Monday, Febru-ary 22. The People's Court (*Volksgerichthof*) was estab-lished by the Nazis in 1934 to try cases of treason and subversion—that is, to eradicate the enemies of National Socialism—and to act as an instrument of terror. Oper-ating outside the realm of German constitutional law, it dealt summary justice, meting out death sentences frequently. The presiding judge of the People's Court, Roland Freisler, who had become notorious as Hitler's "hanging judge," was brought in from Berlin for the occasion. The urgency of the trial and the selection of Freisler signaled that the Nazis were not taking the situ-ation lightly. The trial proceedings consisted mostly of Judge Freisler's berserk tirades against the accused—Hans, Sophie, and Christoph. To Leo Samberger, a young lawyer who witnessed the proceedings from the doorway of the courtroom, it seemed that Freisler's overall tendency was to represent the defendants as a cross between fools and criminals.[174] He denounced, abused, and ridiculed them, breaking out at times into shrieks and screams, and accompanying his outbursts with wild gestures. The court-appointed defense attorneys sat by mutely.

No witnesses were called, because the defendants had confessed to everything. Only occasionally did they get a chance to speak. In contrast to Freisler, their bearing was calm and dignified. Their answers to his outrageous invective, recalled Samberger, were "composed, lucid and bold. . . . There stood people who were manifestly suffused by their ideals."[175] At one point, Sophie was able to interject a comment into Freisler's harangue: "What we wrote and said is what many people are thinking," she declared. "They just don't dare to say it out loud. Somebody, after all, had to make a start."[176]

As the trial was coming to a close, a commotion arose. The Scholl parents, who had been notified of their children's arrest by Traute Lafrenz and Jürgen Wittenstein, had come by train from Ulm. They attempted to make their way into the courtroom, but were hauled out by order of Freisler. Robert Scholl cried out as he was escorted out of the courtroom: "There is a higher justice!" And then added, "They will go down in history!"[177]

After several grueling hours, the show trial came to an end. The verdict: death. Hans turned to Freisler and said, "You will soon stand where we stand now."[178]

Hans's court-appointed defense attorney left the courtroom and approached the Scholl parents, who were waiting outside in the hall. He expressed no condolences or commiseration. Instead, he addressed them with words of reproach for having "brought up their children so badly."[179]

Christoph, Hans, and Sophie were taken to Stadelheim Prison, where the Scholl parents were able to arrange one final meeting with their children. Praying with Hans in his cell, the Protestant prison chaplain read together with him psalms of Hans's own choosing. He administered the Eucharist and then went to attend likewise to Sophie.

Christoph was unable to bid his family farewell. They were unaware of his plight and only learned of his arrest and trial belatedly.[180] The Roman Catholic chaplain came to his cell at Christoph's request and received him into the Catholic Church, afterward administering Christoph's first and last communion. "Now," said Christoph, "my death will be easy and joyful."[181]

Only hours after they had arrived at Stadelheim, Hans, Sophie, and Christoph were taken out of their cells into a smaller building. This was to be the place of their execution. It housed a guillotine, which at about 5 p.m. on February 22, 1943, claimed three young lives: first Sophie, then Christoph, and last Hans. As they neared the final threshold of their earthly lives, Christoph said, "In a few minutes we will meet in eternity." Turning to face the prison, Hans cried out: "Long live freedom!"[182]

The guillotine's work was not done, however.

Criminal Sought:
One Thousand Marks' Reward

Alexander learned of the arrest of the Scholl siblings on the day that they had been taken into custody.[183] A phone call determined that he, too, was under suspicion and that it was not safe for him to go home—the Gestapo had already descended on the Schmorell house and had conducted a search of Alexander's room. He arranged a brief clandestine meeting with Willi Graf to discuss plans for evading the authorities.

Alexander thought it wise to flee Munich. Two close friends helped him prepare for his flight: Nikolai Hamazaspian gave him his Bulgarian passport, and Lilo Ramdohr helped with changing the photograph on it to Alexander's and forging an "official" stamp over it. Hamazaspian also supplied Alexander with a jacket, some food, and money for his escape.

On the morning of February 19, Alexander went to the train station, hoping to meet Willi Graf there. Willi did not show up; however, the station was teeming with police who were checking everyone's documents.

Unbeknownst to Alexander, Willi had been arrested the evening before, together with his sister, Anneliese, who had absolutely no knowledge of her brother's resistance activities. Alexander had to flee alone. He set out late in the evening on February 20. Lilo Ramdohr saw him off. As they parted, Alexander said, "If I manage to get through this all right, then my life will change very much. If not, then I will be glad to die, because I know, after all, that there is no end."[184]

The various accounts of Alexander's flight differ, and it will perhaps never be possible to reconstruct every detail and circumstance connected with it.[185] Traveling at times by train, but mostly on foot to escape detection, Alexander first attempted to go into hiding at a camp of Russian prisoners of war near Innsbruck. There were thousands of people there, and Alexander could lose himself among them. A friend of his, Nadia Konoz (who knew the camp's director), was supposed to meet him at a small train station near Innsbruck and bring him to the camp. She missed the agreed-upon train, however, and came on a later one, only to find that Alexander had already moved on.

Alexander next hoped to enlist the aid of another friend, Ingrid Mesirca, who might have given him refuge

at a health resort in the castle of Elmau, where he had
been a guest in happier times. On Sunday, February 21,
Alexander placed a phone call to Ingrid, but she was
bedridden with a high fever and could not come to his
assistance. Worried about Christoph, and hoping to
determine whether any action had been taken against
him in connection with the Scholls's arrest, Alexander
called Christoph's mother in the town of Tegernsee. It is
not known what news she was able to convey. Alexander
then turned to a Russian coachman he had met on prior
visits to Elmau and was given shelter for two nights in a
haystack on the Elmau estate.

On the afternoon of Tuesday, February 23, two local
policemen who had received orders from Munich came
to Elmau, searching for a certain Alexander Schmorell,
born in Russia in 1917, who was presumed to be in the
vicinity. It is not entirely clear how the Gestapo knew to
look for him there. Perhaps his call to Christoph's mother
had coincided with the Gestapo's confiscation of her radio
(the one on which Christoph had listened to foreign radio
broadcasts) and thus gave a clue to Alexander's whereabouts. Further scraps of evidence indicate that someone among the staff at Elmau had by some means found
out that a search was on for Alexander (they recognized
him from previous visits) and reported him to the local
police. Encountering Alexander at Elmau, the policemen demanded to see his papers. However, they had not
been provided with his physical description, nor did they

detect the falsification of his passport; thus, they did not take him into custody. Still, it was no longer safe to stay in Elmau—he must be on the run again.

If he could get over the Swiss border, he would be safe from Nazi pursuit. That had indeed been one of Alexander's alternatives in his original escape plan as he had outlined it to Hamazaspian. But something made him turn back to Munich. Was it the thought of making a long and difficult trek through snowy mountain passes only to risk being caught by border patrols? Perhaps he was running out of food and money, and felt too physically weary and emotionally exhausted to hazard such a feat. He might have a better chance of lying low in Munich, where he still had friends who had no connection to the White Rose and would not be suspected of harboring him.

Had Christoph's mother given any indication that Christoph was in trouble when Alexander made his call to her? Even if she had not, it can very well be surmised that Alexander just couldn't bring himself to escape to safety while others were being held accountable for actions that they had all undertaken together. In Munich, he would at least be able to find out what was happening to his friends and be ready to take some sort of action.

In the meantime, Alexander had been named as one of the main suspects in the White Rose case on February 19. A search of Alexander's room on that day yielded much incriminating evidence: stencils, carbon paper, absorbent paper that could be used in a duplicating machine, and

ninety-nine postage stamps. The Gestapo presumed that he was on the run, and the borders had been alerted. Then, on February 24, a wanted notice with his photo was printed in three Munich newspapers under the headline "Criminal sought: 1,000 marks reward." Wanted posters were put up throughout the city.

Arriving in Munich at about 10 p.m. on that same day, knowing nothing of the trial or execution of his friends, and unaware that Hans, Sophie, and Christoph had been laid to rest in the cemetery at Perlacher Forst just several hours earlier, Alexander made his way toward the house of an old friend, Marie Luise Upplegger. He would ask her to give him shelter for at least one night.

When he had nearly reached Marie Luise's residence, an air raid siren sounded. Alexander headed for the nearest bomb shelter, knowing that he would find Marie Luise there. Standing at the door of the shelter, he called to her, asking her to come out into the anteroom so that he could speak to her. Worn out from his wanderings, haggard and disheveled, Alexander waited warily. Knowing that he was a wanted man, Marie Luise hesitated, not knowing what to do. To Alexander's surprise, instead of Marie Luise, a man came out and apprehended him. Although he struggled to get free, Alexander was delivered into the hands of the Gestapo not long before midnight.

CHAPTER 14

When? Where? How? With Whom?

The fugitive had become a prisoner. A black Gestapo car sped into the frosty midnight darkness, conveying the arrested Alexander to the Wittelsbach Palace. The palace, once the residence and seat of government of the Bavarian royal family, now housed the Munich headquarters of the Gestapo and a prison.

Alexander had been ceaselessly in hiding or on the run ever since the arrest of the Scholls on February 18—for six unnerving and exhausting days and nights. But the Gestapo, which had initiated its manhunt for him as one of the prime suspects in the White Rose case already on February 20, had no time to waste. The first interrogation began immediately upon Alexander's arrival at the palace. Interrogators began grilling their prey in the wee hours of the night and kept at it round the clock,

with some pauses, throughout two days, February 25 and 26.

During Alexander's flight, the arrested students of the White Rose who had been in uniform were discharged from the army by order of General Field-Marshall Keitel in Berlin and at the behest of Martin Bormann, with the collusion of Gauleiter Giesler.[186] This allowed them to be put under the jurisdiction of the notorious People's Court rather than a military court, thus ensuring, as Bormann's urgent telex to Munich stated, that the proceedings would be carried out as quickly as possible. On February 22 Alexander was expelled from the university and permanently excluded from studying at any other institution of higher learning in Germany. Thus, Alexander faced his interrogators stripped of any rank, and also without any knowledge regarding the fate of any friends or relatives, other than the fact of Hans and Sophie's arrest.

Yet he had the strength of his faith and his convictions to uphold him. From the start, he took a straightforward course, stating openly, firmly, and fearlessly what he had done and what his motivations had been.

The questioning[187] began by establishing facts pertaining to Alexander's birth, background, studies, service in the military, and circle of friends. Very soon however, the attention of the interrogator shifted to Alexander's political orientation. In response, Alexander made statement after statement, any *one* of which would have been enough cause for weighty reprisals.

"I will readily admit that I cannot declare myself to be a National Socialist,"[188] states Alexander unequivocally and without hesitation. He then proceeds to elucidate: Although he rejects Bolshevism as well, he readily acknowledges his love for Russia, the land of his birth. He declares himself to be a monarchist, though only as concerns Russia, not Germany. The war between Germany and Russia causes him "deep pain and sorrow." He would gladly see this war quickly brought to an end, with Russia suffering as few losses as possible.

Alexander discloses the inner moral conflict he experienced in connection with swearing an oath of personal allegiance to Hitler upon joining the army, which led him to request a discharge. He tells his interrogator that, after his request for discharge was denied, he "continued to wear the uniform of the German soldier reluctantly."

While in Russia, serving as a medical officer on the Eastern front in the summer of 1942, he was fortunate not to bear arms. There "I did not encounter any situation where my disposition toward Russia could have been detrimental to Germany's interests." At the same time, had he been given the order to shoot at Russians, "I would have felt obliged to notify my superiors that I could not do so."

Lest his family be adversely implicated in his views, Alexander makes sure to assert that "as a German, my father was aggrieved by my attitude toward Russia. . . .

Lately we have even come to having minor quarrels about this." As a final touch to this part of the interrogation, Alexander mentions something that would have been highly repugnant to Nazi ears: from Russian prisoners, he had repeatedly heard that German successes in the war were attributable chiefly to the treason of Russian generals.

Now the interrogation gets down to eliciting facts actually pertaining to the case.[189] Alexander's complicity in the activities of the White Rose circle had already been quite firmly established even before his arrest: first, by the search of his room, which yielded unquestionably incriminating evidence; second, by his own flight; and, finally, by the interrogations of Hans Scholl, who had started out by taking full and sole responsibility but had been forced to disclose some of Alexander's involvement as he was presented with incontrovertible evidence of such. The interrogators set out to establish not only the full extent of Alexander's own role in the "treasonous" activities of the White Rose, but also to extract from him as much as possible regarding the details of "when? where? how?" and, most important, "with whom?"

Again Alexander proceeds with forthright directness. He freely admits to his part in writing, reproducing, and disseminating the leaflets of the White Rose and in painting anti-Nazi slogans on the walls of Munich buildings. Going back to the summer of 1942, when he and Hans had finally decided to write the first leaflet, he

recounts and takes upon himself the responsibility for all phases of the White Rose actions: the writing of the first draft, typing the leaflet, purchasing paper and a duplicating machine, producing hundreds of copies, writing out addresses from telephone directories, procuring and addressing envelopes, distributing the leaflets in Munich and traveling to other cities to mail them there. The nocturnal painting of graffiti likewise is disclosed by Alexander without any attempts at evasion.

While denying nothing in respect to his own involvement, Alexander downplays or conceals the activities of others—especially those who, he hoped, had not yet fallen into the hands of the Gestapo—and diligently attempts to divert any suspicions that might fall on anyone besides himself and Hans: "We were especially careful to prevent it from becoming known amongst our friends that we were the publishers of these leaflets," he declares. "No one other than Scholl and myself was present while we were typing."[190] Regarding Traute Lafrenz, Alexander asserts that she "came by the Scholl siblings' apartment often, but I do not believe that they informed her of our treasonous propaganda. I am only casually acquainted with Miss Lafrenz, and would be wary of confiding in her."[191]

Alexander firmly maintains that his family knew nothing of the leaflets or their production: "At my parents' home, where I have my own room on the third floor, we conducted ourselves in such a way that it was impossible for my parents to notice anything." The typewriter

upon which the leaflets were typed belonged to a friend. When asking to borrow it, "I misled him by saying that I needed it for a school assignment." As for funding the operation, "The costs of producing the leaflets we [Hans and Alexander] have borne jointly."

The students had done an about-face. If prior to their capture they had sought to give the impression of a wide network of conspirators and collaborators, Alexander, Hans, and Sophie fervently tried to convince their Nazi captors that the whole operation—which had, after all, involved dozens of people—had been carried out by one or two active participants, with one or two inadvertent bystanders.

Alexander rather tersely summed up the reasons for his and Hans's activities: "This action can be considered consonant with our political outlook. At that time, we saw so-called passive resistance and acts of sabotage as the only feasible means of putting an end to the war."

As regards painting "Down with Hitler!" and "Hitler is a mass murderer" on city walls: "With these graffiti, we wished to address our propaganda generally to the people en masse, which was impossible for us to accomplish to this degree through the dissemination of leaflets."

And, in conclusion, the last paragraph of the interrogation of February 25 states:

Through the publication and dissemination of our leaflets, Hans Scholl and I wanted to bring about an upheaval.

We were fully aware that our course of action was directed against the present regime, and that if we were caught, we would have to face the harshest penalties. However, that did not prevent us from acting against the present regime in such manner, because we were both convinced that we could thus shorten the war.

What was Sophie's role in the affair? Alexander declares, "I can only say that she was not allowed to take any significant part in it." This statement is recorded in the very beginning paragraph of the interrogation transcript of February 25. But the Gestapo was adept at its nefarious job. Pages—and what must have been many hours and untold sufferings—later, near the end of the same interrogation, we read the following: "When I am questioned regarding the involvement of Sophie Scholl in our treasonous propaganda, I truthfully state that she traveled to Augsburg at the same time as I did, in order to disseminate the leaflet entitled *A Call to All Germans*. I know nothing about her going from Augsburg to any other cities."

By this time, Alexander must have been given to understand that he could no longer shield Sophie completely. At this point, his only recourse was to give out no further information regarding other cities from which Sophie had posted leaflets and to cover up for those of Sophie's friends, such as the Hirzel siblings, who had assisted her in distributing the White Rose flyers.

One can only surmise what anguish this admission of Sophie's involvement cost him, and what tactics had been used to wrest this admission from him. (It is unclear when Alexander learned of the Scholls's execution. It is likely that at this point, he still thought they were alive.)

The interrogation continued into the next day, February 26.[192] The transcript of this ordeal begins with the words: "Brought forth from prison, Alexander Schmorell stated the following." Alexander reiterates statements he had already made regarding the train of thought and the events that had brought him to the point at which he "could no longer be content to remain a silent opponent of National Socialism." He was driven by his deep concern both for Germany and for Russia and felt compelled to act by a sense of duty to both countries. But he insists that his actions were not aimed at aiding and abetting the enemy at the expense of German military might.

Now the Gestapo turns its attention to the chain of events surrounding his flight from Munich. Again, Alexander divulges selected facts but conceals or falsifies information that could incriminate his comrades. He "stole" Hamazaspian's passport while the latter left the room for a short time, and then he substituted his own photo for Hamazaspian's and forged a stamp over it.[193] Not one word did he say regarding Lilo Ramdohr's help in this matter or of the fact that she sheltered him during his first night as a fugitive ("I slept that night in the English Gardens").

There is more probing about his youth, about people, objects, and events. When confronted with evidence or accusations of which he was not guilty, Alexander sets the record straight. He has never heard of that person, he does not know anything about this yellow envelope. And "the supposition that I am connected with Russian individuals or agencies for purposes of transmitting information is incorrect. I must categorically defend myself against such a charge, as there is absolutely no basis for it."

The interrogation of February 26 ends with Alexander's pronouncement: "I confess to high treason, however I deny having acted as a traitor to my country."[194]

At least four more interrogations took place in the space of the next three weeks—on March 1, 11, 13, and 18.[195] These interrogations seem to have been shorter than those of February 25 and 26 (if one is to judge by the length of the transcripts). One matter that evidently concerned the Gestapo was the question of outside influence on the young people and their undertakings. In this regard, Alexander makes it a point to say that, although he is a devoutly believing member of the Russian Orthodox Church, "no clergymen or other church officials have anything to do with our subversive activity."

Several interrogation transcripts include questions posed by the interrogating agent. The first one of March 1 is chilling: "Would you now finally like to make precise declarations regarding who composed, revised or

distributed the individual leaflets?" Some information must have been unearthed since the last interrogation, which had exposed the untruth of some of Alexander's "evidence."

In the meantime, the Gestapo had not been idle elsewhere. Hans and Susanne Hirzel had fallen into the hands of the Gestapo several days prior to Alexander's capture. On the day following Alexander's arrest, his parents and siblings were taken into *Sippenhaft* (clan custody). Professor Huber was seized on February 27.[196] Others followed; Angelika Probst, Lilo Ramdohr, Falk Harnack, Traute Lafrenz, Eugen Grimminger, and other friends and relatives of the White Rose circle began to fill the cells of the city's prisons. Some were released upon questioning; quite a few others remained in custody. The Schmorells spent more than three weeks behind bars, with the threat of internment in a concentration camp hanging over them.

The knowledge that his friends and loved ones were being subjected to imprisonment and interrogation must have exponentially increased Alexander's distress—a tool the Gestapo was known to use readily to its advantage. Moreover, there is reason to believe that the Gestapo did not stop at employing solely psychological means of exerting pressure on him. Harnack's account of glimpsing Alexander being escorted down the corridor of the prison with his "face inflamed and his eyes as burning holes,"[197] and something Alexander said to a codefendant after the trial ("If you only knew what I've gone through and what

they did to me.")[198] have led both Alexander's family and chroniclers of the White Rose to infer that the Gestapo interrogators applied extreme physical means to achieve their ends with Alexander. For although the Scholls and the Schmorell parents and siblings were not mistreated during their imprisonment, it must be remembered that Alexander had Slavic blood (or, in Nazi parlance, the blood of *Untermenschen*) in his veins.[199]

On March 25, exactly a month into his ordeal, Alexander was transferred from the Wittelsbach Palace to Neudeck Prison for investigative custody. After questioning in front of a judge, during which he repeated his previous testimonies to the Gestapo, Alexander affirmed in writing that he had participated with Hans and Sophie Scholl in publishing and distributing the leaflets of the "Resistance Movement in Germany" as well as the leaflets of the "White Rose." He also admitted to painting inflammatory slogans on the walls of the university.

Thereupon the judge issued a warrant for commitment to prison, as the accused was "strongly suspected" of high treason, aiding and abetting the enemy, and undermining military morale. Although the authorities had acted swiftly in the case of Hans, Sophie, and Christoph, Alexander would languish in prison for weeks before he and thirteen others were brought to trial by the People's Court on April 19.

CHAPTER 15

Before the People's Court

Alexander's plight caused consternation for his entire family. Remembering the swiftness and ruthlessness of the summary justice dealt to Hans, Sophie, and Christoph, the family attempted to intervene with the authorities on his behalf. On March 17, even before Alexander's formal commitment to prison, his uncle Rudolf Hoffmann (brother of Alexander's stepmother, Elisabeth) directed a petition for clemency to Heinrich Himmler. Hoffmann and his two brothers, who cosigned the petition, were members of the Nazi Party in good standing and hoped that their influence might save their nephew from sharing the fate of the Scholls.

Alexander's parents were themselves in prison at this time. They were released on March 20, and on March 22, they likewise addressed a clemency petition to Himmler.

On the very day that Alexander was committed to prison (March 25), the Schmorells applied for permission to visit Alexander and bring him some groceries. Permission was denied. However, one meeting between Alexander and his parents did take place during the term of his imprisonment.[200]

Himmler replied to Hoffman in a letter dated April 11.[201] He rejected Hoffman's plea for clemency, and offered instead to give him access to Alexander's investigative files that he might see for himself that his nephew's "reprehensible crime, which is surely to be attributed largely to his part-Russian blood, has merited a just punishment." "Furthermore," continued Himmler, "at a time when thousands of worthy Germans are risking their lives for the sake of the Fatherland, it would be unjustifiable to commute the execution of the death penalty." The letter concluded with chilling words: "Occasionally an unworthy individual might be found within a family. However, it is then necessary that this person be eliminated from the national and family community!"[202]

Thus, the death sentence had already been determined *prior to* the trial, which took place on April 19.

Falk Harnack, who was to stand trial with Alexander, remembered the days before the trial thus:

> Because the case was being brought before the People's Court, where no penal code had any legal force, but rather only arbitrariness ruled, each one of us prepared ourselves for the death

penalty. Slowly one overcame the fear of death. Only one emotion plagued all of us: the thought of not having done enough against the villainous system. One had the feeling that one was giving up one's life too cheaply.[203]

The three main defendants in the trial were Alexander Schmorell, Willi Graf, and Kurt Huber. For their "treacherous and nefarious" activities, they were charged with high treason.

Eleven others—friends and supporters of the White Rose—were also tried with them. The siblings Susanne and Hans Hirzel had disseminated White Rose leaflets, aided by Hans's high school classmates Franz Müller and Heinrich Guter. Eugen Grimminger had donated money to the cause. Heinz Bollinger and Helmut Bauer of Freiburg had been linked to Willi Graf's resistance activities. Falk Harnack and three friends of Sophie Scholl—Traute Lafrenz, Gisela Schertling, and Katharina Schüddekopf—had knowledge of the White Rose leaflet campaign, but did not report it to the authorities. All of the accused, with the exception of Professor Huber, Grimminger, and Harnack, were either college students in their early twenties or high school students in their teens.

On the morning of April 19, the fourteen defendants were woken early. They were escorted from their cells into a green paddy wagon, which went from prison to prison, picking them up by groups. When the portal of

the prison opened, Susanne Hirzel saw a long, golden beam of sunshine—it was springtime. The paddy wagon wended its way through the city; Susanne was able to catch glimpses of trees, blooming bushes, and city streets, wet and glistening. After weeks of incarceration, her joy at this contact with the outside world and nature made the day's beginning seem like a holiday.[204]

At last all fourteen were seated in the van. This was the first time in months that many of them had seen each other. Some had never met before. "The mood in the van was grave," Harnack remembered, "and yet there prevailed a feeling of profound harmony among us all."

The prisoners were brought to the Palace of Justice, where just two months earlier the Scholl siblings and Christoph Probst had been tried and sentenced to death. They were greeted by a cordon of police then escorted to a barred waiting room. Each was assigned a guard who escorted his charge throughout the day. Harnack continues: "We were able to exchange only a few phrases, because we were closely guarded. Schmorell was silent; he hoped for nothing."

Then they were led—the men handcuffed, the women grasped by the hand—through the corridors of the Palace of Justice to a rather small courtroom.[205] "To the left and right," narrates Harnack, "stood people, shoulder to shoulder—numerous students from the University of Munich, workers, soldiers. As we passed by them, we

were met with no disheartening words, only glances full of sympathy and compassion."

Alexander entered the courtroom first; then came Professor Huber, followed by the rest of the defendants. The courtroom was packed with members of the Nazi Party and the Gestapo, officers in uniform, and even two generals. The mayor of Munich was present, along with other high-ranking officials. The mood in the courtroom was the opposite of that which the defendants had encountered in the corridor. To Harnack, it seemed that "the brown party big-shots would gladly have jumped up and given us a beating."

Once the defendants were seated, five judges entered the courtroom, led by Roland Freisler, who had again arrived from Berlin to preside over the People's Court. The names of the accused were read aloud, along with the charges against them, Alexander's name leading the list. Then the names of the defendants' lawyers were announced (Hugo Schmorell had secured the attorney Siegfried Deisinger to represent Alexander), although their role was to be rather minimal.

Thus began the second trial of the White Rose. Freisler conducted it as he had the first White Rose trial—with diabolically calculated theatrics. He screamed, whispered, and gesticulated wildly; he demeaned, degraded, and berated the defendants, interrupting them with his hysterical outbursts. Susanne Hirzel noted that "he angrily unleashed his contempt, scorn and ridicule most

particularly against Alex Schmorell and Professor Huber. He tried to make them look ludicrous and reviled them viciously."

Alexander was the first to be called up for cross-examination. "Freisler deluged the young student with bestial rhetoric, heaping insult upon insult, raging, so that Schmorell could hardly say anything," recounts Harnack, "Every time that he attempted to explain his actions, to defend himself, Freisler would cut him off with his screaming." When he had finally vented much of his fury, Freisler asked Alexander what he had done at the front. "I took care of the wounded, which was my duty as medical orderly," answered Alexander. As regards shooting Russians, "I would no more readily shoot a Russian than I would shoot a German." This provoked a new barrage of invective from Freisler: "Look at this traitor who is supposed to be a German sergeant! He is stabbing his Fatherland in the back!"

At one point, according to Susanne Hirzel, when Alexander referred to "Professor Huber," Freisler exploded: "I know no Professor Huber, nor a Dr. Huber! I know only the accused Huber, who does not deserve to be a German, because he is a reprobate!"

After more such interchanges, Alexander was dismissed, and others were in their turn subjected to Freisler's venom.

The trial lasted from 9 a.m. until 11 p.m.—some fourteen hours—with a half-hour break. While others left for

lunch, the defendants remained in the courtroom and a one-liter jug of water was brought in for their refreshment, along with a tin container of carrots, which they ate standing up. Susanne Hirzel overheard Professor Huber say to Falk Harnack: "Isn't this a sorry picture, this so-called People's Court? Isn't this a disgrace for the German people?" And Susanne herself wondered why not one person in the courtroom had called out: "Where is justice?"

The defendants' lawyers were given the opportunity to speak, each attempting a cautious defense and plea for a milder sentence, but this was merely an empty formality.

Then came the turn of the defendants themselves to say one final word in their own behalf. Professor Huber delivered a lengthy speech (interrupted periodically by snarling comments from Freisler) in which he eloquently set forth the motives for his actions and his beliefs. He was a German patriot, and his resistance had stemmed from his belief that it was a person's moral duty to oppose a corrupt state that criminally trampled on human rights. Huber expressed his desire that Germany should "return to its basic values, to a state based on legality, to a return of trust between man and man,"[206] and voiced his hope that Germany would soon recover its spiritual freedom.

Alexander and Willi once more briefly reasserted their deliberate share in the actions of the White Rose. Alexander expressed no regret for what he had done.

In Harnack's recollection, "Schmorell and Graf remained calm and collected, and admitted their illegal activities, which they had undertaken out of their belief in a better Germany."

Late in the evening, Freisler adjourned the proceedings and left the courtroom with the other judges to consider the verdicts. The thick gruel that was offered to the defendants as a repast remained untouched. They paced the room anxiously.

Finally, the judges returned. Freisler read the words of the judgment:

> *Alexander Schmorell, Kurt Huber, and Wilhelm Graf have, in time of war, produced leaflets urging sabotage of the war effort and the overthrow of the National Socialist way of life; they have also spread defeatist ideas, and vilified the Führer in the grossest manner; all of which aided and abetted the enemies of the Reich and undermined the fighting capacity of our nation.*
>
> *They are therefore condemned to death.*[207]

Then the verdicts of the other defendants were pronounced: Eugen Grimminger, ten years; Heinz Bollinger and Helmut Bauer, seven years; Hans Hirzel and Franz Müller, five years. The rest, mostly young women, received between six and eighteen months, with the exception of Harnack, who was acquitted.[208] The three who had just heard the pronouncement of their death sentence remained serene, silent, and composed.

Freisler left the courtroom, and the sentenced "criminals" were escorted into the paddy wagon, which was waiting to take them to Stadelheim Prison on the outskirts of Munich. Harnack recalls that "Professor Huber sat quietly, withdrawn into himself. Schmorell and Graf sympathized keenly with him."

For Traute Lafrenz, this trip was unforgettable:

> It was like after a celebration. Most of us had spent long weeks in solitary confinement, and I remember that, despite the three death sentences, we talked loudly and excitedly, and even laughed. Professor Huber showed photos of his children. We consoled each other with the thought that condemned men were granted 99 days, and that by then the war could very well be lost and ended.[209]

It was midnight when they arrived in the courtyard of Stadelheim. The prison gates creaked. Reality dawned as the fourteen got out of the van. "It was horrible," recalled Traute. "Each one of us knew that we would not see each other for a very long time—if ever."[210]

The prisoners were met by a guard who proceeded to sort them, as Harnack put it, "like wares in a store." Death sentence, to the right corner; penitentiary, to the left corner; and prison, on the other side.

It was time for good-byes. To Harnack, "the parting was indescribable. This 'farewell' of all fourteen is something that one can never forget."

Harnack was told to go with the condemned men. They walked down endless brightly lit corridors, until they reached death row. Tablets on each cell door bore the letters "TU" for *Todesurteil* (death sentence). Outside each cell were parcels of clothing—the condemned slept naked, their hands in handcuffs.

A few brief but heartfelt words of farewell, and the four were taken to their respective cells. Harnack found himself alone, his head spinning. The whole night, he could not sleep and paced to and fro, kept awake by distressing thoughts. What was happening to his friends? As the night dragged on, his overwrought imagination transformed every little sound into the thud of the guillotine. Hadn't Hans, Sophie, and Christoph been executed on the very day of their trial?

Elsewhere, in another prison, Hugo Schmorell was thinking similar thoughts. The Schmorell parents had once again been taken into custody by the Gestapo on April 15. The reason: a "subversive cast of mind," evidenced by the fact that they had "dared" to address a clemency petition to Himmler. They were released after three weeks because Elisabeth Schmorell fell seriously ill as a result of emotional trauma, and the prison doctor pronounced her unfit to remain in confinement.[211] On April 21, two days after the sentencing, Hugo wrote a letter to the chief prosecutor of the People's Court. Fearing that the death penalty would be carried out as swiftly as it had been after the first White Rose trial, he asked

that, should the verdict be executed, Alexander's body be released to the family for burial.[212]

But Hugo's fears did not materialize immediately. For Alexander, Willi, and Professor Huber, there was to be no frenzied hurry on the part of the Nazis to execute them, as had been the case for the first threesome. Instead, they awaited death for days, then weeks, and then months. In the words of Fr Ferdinand Brinkmann, the Catholic prison chaplain who visited the three during their incarceration, this agonizing ordeal made Stadelheim Prison their Golgotha.[213]

Setting a Course for Heaven

In 1943, Easter for both western Christians and Eastern Orthodox Christians fell on April 25. And thus it happened that April 19, the day of Alexander's trial, was the first day of Holy Week—Great and Holy Monday, the day that the Church sings: "Today Christ in His love hastens to His suffering."[214] Quoting Christ, a hymn of the day says: "Ye shall drink the cup that I drink of, and so ye shall be glorified with Me in the Kingdom of the Father." Perhaps it was no coincidence that on that very day, Alexander received his death sentence and hastened forth on the final journey of his own suffering.

In compline of Great Monday we find the following words: "Thou hast heard my soul, how Christ spoke in prophecy to his holy disciples, foretelling the consummation of all things. Make ready then, since thou knowest

that the end will come; the hour of departure is at hand."
One of Alexander's first steps in "making ready" concerned Marie Luise Upplegger, whom he suspected as
having been the cause of his arrest in the Munich air-raid
shelter on February 24. Turning to his friends immediately after the trial, he expressed his hope that Marie Luise
would suffer no reprisals should she be called to account
after the fall of Hitler's regime. He reiterated this sentiment some time later, asking his lawyer to ensure that no
harm would come to Marie Luise.

What were those days of incarceration like for Alexander? Did he hope for a happier outcome to his ordeal,
that his death sentence would not be carried out? It is
quite conceivable that he did. There was the possibility
that the war would come to a speedy end and that the
resulting fall of the Nazis would bring liberation to those
who were unjustly imprisoned.

And yet, to Fr Ferdinand Brinkmann, it seemed
that Alexander had no illusions or false hopes as to what
awaited him—that, from the first day of his confinement
on death row, Alexander had "set a course for heaven."[215]

Alexander's lawyer, Siegfried Deisinger, was able to
visit him in prison and was surprised to find his young
client calm and composed. He came away with the
impression that a source of solace for Alexander was the
unwavering conviction that he had acted for a right and
true cause. Deisinger wrote: "Even in the last weeks of his
life, Alex Schmorell never lost his self-possession or the

confidence that what he had done was right. It was distressing to see this young man, so obviously gifted and full of promise, standing before me with so terrible a doom upon him; but where I was shaken, he was serene and even lighthearted."[216]

Yet there was an even deeper source of consolation for Alexander. Reminiscing about her incarceration after the trial of April 19, Susanne Hirzel wrote that those endless and monotonous days afforded her a time of unhampered self-examination.[217] We can reasonably assume that, during his imprisonment, Alexander likewise underwent a process of introspection and spiritual maturation that might be called a "secret inner ripening,"[218] during which "out of weakness [he was] made strong."[219] In the many pages of his published correspondence, Alexander is reticent about spiritual matters; he seems hesitant to divulge his own spiritual sentiments or experiences. It is from letters that he was allowed to write home from prison (a total of seven)[220] that we are finally afforded a glimpse into the workings of Alexander's soul, as he sought—and obtained—profound and ultimate consolation in his faith.

The first letter was written on the Saturday after Easter, May 1.[221]

Dear Parents,

There is of course not much that is new to write you about; here one day is much like another and time passes very rapidly. Dear Father, dear Mother, if I have to die now, you must know

that I am not at all afraid of death—regarding that you need have no concern. After all, I know that a better life awaits us and will bring us all together again.[222] *The thing that is hard for me is to have to leave all of you whom I have loved so much and who have loved me so much. How much I have loved you I realize only now at the parting, when I must lose all of you. Try to overcome the pain of losing me, do not forget that there is a fate, that this fate did not allot a longer life to me, and that therefore this had to come about as it did. And nothing happens contrary to the will of God.*

My greeting to everyone, my most heartfelt greeting to all. I embrace you and kiss all of you many times over.

Your Shurik

The days dragged on, yet the end and, with it, the dreaded separation from loved ones did not come. There was still the matter of clemency petitions for the three condemned men—Alexander, Willi Graf, and Professor Huber. Efforts to obtain pardon or leniency were made on behalf of the professor through civilian channels; they eventually came to naught. The case of Alexander and Willi was more complicated. A protracted bureaucratic dispute between civilian and military authorities took place, each claiming jurisdiction over the two young non-commissioned officers. Who had the final say regarding a possible decision to pardon them: the Reich Ministry of Justice or the High Command of the Armed Forces? While the authorities wrangled, the prisoners waited and

sought refuge and sustenance in the One who had the ultimate authority over them.

In his second letter, dated May 30, Alexander wrote to his family to comfort them with his deepening insight. He had found a way to overcome the pain of the impending separation from those he loved, the pain that he feared more than death:

> *In case my plea for mercy is rejected, remember that "death" does not mean the end of all life, but actually, on the contrary, a birth, a passing over into a new life, a glorious and everlasting life. Hence death is not a fearful thing. It is the separation that is hard, and heavy to bear. But it becomes less hard and less heavy to bear when we remain mindful that we are indeed not parting forever, but only for a time—as for a journey—in order afterward to meet again for ever and always in a life that is infinitely more beautiful than the present one, and that then there will be no end of our being together. Remember all this and your burden will surely become lighter.*

Two more weeks went by—quickly, it seemed to Alexander. Realizing that his family might be anxious not only about his state of mind, but also about his physical well-being, on June 5 he wrote: "Things are well for me. My health is fine and I am in good spirits. There's nothing new here. I read a lot—I've gotten hold of some very good books. And I can sleep as much as I like—11 to 12 hours—so there's no lack of that. Every other day I go for

a one-hour walk; yesterday I even bathed." He hopes that all are likewise well at home and that his loved ones have attained some measure of consolation and then exhorts: "Do not abandon hope for a reunion here on earth or beyond in eternity. God arranges everything according to His will, and for our good. We must simply always place ourselves trustingly in His hands, and then He will never forsake us, but will always help and console us."[223]

An escape plan had been devised for Alexander by Nikolai Hamazaspian and his friend Georg Schlee. (This may be what the "hope for reunion here on earth" referred to.) Schlee, a court interpreter, knew a guard at Stadelheim Prison who was critical of the Nazis and who could be persuaded to play a crucial part in the following projected scenario, related years later by Hamazaspian: "The prison guard would enter Schmorell's cell, Schmorell would knock him out, and then flee. I had scouted around for a place near the prison where we could hide a bicycle and some clothes for Shurik for his flight." Alexander rejected this plan, however, because he did not want to save his own life by endangering the life of another.[224]

Alexander wrote next on June 18, once again with the intention to ease the sorrow of his loved ones. From a fellow prisoner, he had received books of a spiritual nature that moved him deeply. He wrote: "Recently I read in a very good and significant book a passage that applies very well to you: 'The greater the tragic element in life, the greater our faith must be; the more we seem forsaken by

God, the more confidently must we give our souls into the Father's hands.'" And he continued,

> The holy abbot Theodore of Byzantium[225] wrote: "And there I have given thanks to God for misfortune and bowed to the unfathomable decrees of his providence, which from the founding of the world has purposefully foreseen the time and place of each man's death." That is just about what I have already written you. It would make me very happy if you thought likewise: it would take so much sadness and sorrow from you. But I haven't died yet—so pray and don't lose hope.

Though trying to console his loved ones with the possibility of a reprieve, Alexander had no misconceptions as to his impending fate. On that same day he wrote a letter to Nelly, a young lady residing in Russia whom he had met while stationed there the previous summer. "Dear Nelly," he wrote, "earlier than we all thought it has been fated for me to leave the earthly life." Taking leave of her, and through her, perhaps, bidding farewell to his beloved Russia, he ends thus: "In the next, the eternal life, we will meet again. Farewell, dear Nelly! And pray for me!" This letter, written on the inside of an envelope that had originally enclosed a letter to Alexander from his stepmother, had to be smuggled out of prison because it was against regulations to write to a nonrelative—especially in Russian. Because the Russian Army had retaken Gzhatsk, the city where Nelly lived, it was

impossible to mail her the letter. Returned to the Schmorell family sometime later, it remains the only letter from
prison preserved in Alexander's own hand.[226]

By the end of June, the clemency petition for Alexander and Willi had passed through the various echelons of
the military until it reached the highest level, the Führer
himself. On June 25, as the supreme commander of the
Wehrmacht, Hitler pronounced the final and conclusive
decision: "I reject this appeal for mercy. Adolf Hitler."

Alexander was not apprised of this.

Do Not Forget God!

As Alexander languished in prison, his inner peace unfolded further, contrasting sharply with the mood expressed in letters he had written during the winter prior to his arrest, complaining that "bleakness and sadness have become my constant companions," and that "dreadful disquiet is the prevailing characteristic of my life," with no respite of calm. Now, after having spent over four months in prison, and almost three months on death row, he was moved to write the following letter to his sister.

July 2, 1943

My dear, dear Natasha:

You have surely read the letters I have written to our parents, so that you are fairly well posted. You will perhaps be surprised when I tell you that I am day by day becoming calmer inwardly,

even joyous and glad, and that my mood is nearly always better than it used to be when I was free! How does this happen? I'll tell you at once. This whole terrible "misfortune" has been necessary to show me the right way—and therefore it has actually not been a misfortune at all. Above all, I am glad, and grateful to God for it, that it has been granted to me to understand this sign from Him, and thereby to find the right way. For what did I know before this of faith, of true, deep faith, of truth, of the ultimate and only truth of God? Very little!

But now I have progressed so far that I am happy and calm and confident even in my present situation—come what may. I hope that you have experienced a similar development and that you too, after the deep sorrow of separation, have reached the point of thanking God for everything. *This misfortune was necessary; it opened my eyes—not only my eyes but also the eyes of all those whom it has befallen, our family included.*

I hope that all of you have likewise understood correctly this sign from God. My sincerest greetings to all, but greetings especially to you from.

Your Shurik

During her imprisonment by the Gestapo, Natasha had nearly lost sight in one eye as a result of a retinal detachment. Having received news of this, Alexander asked for permission to write a letter home without waiting for the requisite number of weeks to elapse. In a short note dated July 11, ever solicitous of the welfare of others, he urged his parents to make sure that his sister received

the best of care. He cautioned against going to the medical clinic at the university—"I know how they work there"—and expressed hope that Natasha is being treated by Professor Wessely: "He is the best eye specialist." Alexander advised Natasha to follow her doctor's prescribed treatment exactly to make sure that it is successful.

A few days earlier, on July 8, unbeknownst to Alexander, the senior prosecutor in Munich had advised the chief prosecutor of the People's Court in Berlin that the day of the executions of Alexander Schmorell and Professor Kurt Huber was set for Tuesday, July 13. Willi Graf, however, was still required for further questioning, and his execution was postponed.

Early on the morning of July 13, Alexander received the official order of execution. It was to take place at 5 p.m. that afternoon, with Alexander going first, followed by Professor Huber. Alexander picked up his pen one last time to write his loved ones a letter of farewell.

Dear Mother and Father,

It was indeed not to be otherwise, and by the will of God I am to conclude my earthly life today, in order to enter upon a new life that will never end, and in which we shall all meet again. May this reunion be your comfort and your hope. Unfortunately, this blow is harder to bear for you than for me, for I leave this life with the knowledge that I have served my deepest conviction and the truth. All this permits me to face the approaching hour of death with a calm conscience.

Think of the millions of young men who are giving up their lives on the battlefield—their fate is also mine. Greet all those who are dear to my heart most affectionately! But especially Natasha, Erich, Nyanya, Aunt Toni, Maria, Alionushka and Andrey.

In a few hours I shall be in the better world, with my mother; I shall not forget you, and shall intercede with God for your solace and peace. And I shall wait for you. One thing above all I urge upon you[227]: do not forget God!!!

Your Shurik

With me goes Professor Huber, who also sends his heartfelt greetings!

At midday, Fr Alexander (Lovchii), who had been summoned by Siegfried Deisinger, came to hear Alexander's last confession and to administer Holy Communion.[228] Not long after, when Deisinger entered the cell, Alexander met him almost joyfully. "In the death cell," wrote Deisinger,

I encountered one who had just received the last comforting gifts of his religion[229] and who had already cast from himself all earthly things. Unforgettable are the words he spoke serenely to me: "You will be surprised that I am so calm at such a moment. But I can tell you that even if you told me right now that someone else had offered to die in my place—for instance, my prison guard—I would nonetheless choose to die. I am convinced that my life must end now, early as it seems, because I have fulfilled my mission in life, and I cannot imagine what else I would do in this world if I were set free right now."[230]

Then it was time for Deisinger to leave the cell, as the hour of death was drawing near and the final preparations for the execution had begun. "Firmly and courageously Alexander bid farewell to me. His final greeting was for his family. There emanated from him such a true and profound son's and brother's love, which completely filled him."[231]

There was one final delay. As 5 p.m. drew near, three SS officers arrived unexpectedly at Stadelheim bearing papers that gave them permission to be present at the execution (a highly irregular occurrence). They had hoped to witness a hanging to determine how long it took for a man to strangle to death, and whether the process could be shortened or prolonged at will. Disappointed by the fact that there was to be a beheading instead, they requested that they be shown the workings of the guillotine. Their visit, and the detailed explanation they received, delayed the execution.

To Deisinger, this macabre episode underlined the stark contrast between Alexander and the surrounding abomination. "On the one side was idealism and the moral stature of a young man prepared to die for it. On the other side were those subhuman types with their obscene desire to watch death being inflicted upon a defenseless victim."[232]

The delay, however, did not cause Alexander to falter. With dignity he walked across the prison courtyard to a small barrack containing the guillotine that had claimed

his friends' lives and was about to claim his.[233] Firmly and loudly resounded his "Yes" in the gloomy death chamber when the prosecutor on duty asked him whether he was Alexander Schmorell. Seconds later, he passed over into that "new life, the glorious and everlasting life" which he so fervently spoke of in his letters and of which, throughout his last weeks on earth, he "had been persuaded, and which he had embraced," having come to feel himself "a stranger and pilgrim on the earth."[234]

He was followed several minutes later by Professor Huber.

The day was July 13, the feast day of the Holy Apostles, most of whom had suffered martyric deaths.[235] The funeral was conducted by Fr Alexander on the evening of the next day. Only a close circle of family members was permitted to be present. Alexander was laid to rest in the cemetery at Perlacher Forst, not far from Hans, Sophie, and Christoph.

Nikolai Hamazaspian watched from a distance. On his way to the cemetery he had passed a poster announcing the execution of the "traitors Professor Huber and Alexander Schmorell." Across the poster, in bold letters, someone had written: "Their spirit lives!"[236]

CHAPTER 18

You Shall Not Have Died in Vain

At the time of his death on July 13, 1943, Alexander Schmorell was just two months shy of his twenty-sixth birthday. He would have finished his medical studies in the summer of that year and become a doctor. As it was, he spent what would have been his last semester of studies in prison, growing, instead, in knowledge of things spiritual and healing his own soul.

It is impossible to imagine the grief that engulfed the Schmorell household upon Alexander's death. We are afforded a glimpse into these sorrowful days through the reminiscences of Elisabeth Scholl-Hartnagel, the youngest sister of Sophie and Hans. "After Alex's death," she recalled, "we would call his parents every time we came to Munich to visit the gravesite of Hans and Sophie. Several times we met with Alex's parents at the cemetery."

 136

During one such meeting of the bereaved families, the Scholls found out something that, in Elisabeth Hartnagel's estimation, made the Schmorells's plight even harder than their own.

> There, Schmorell's stepmother related to us that they were forced to sign a statement saying that they considered Alex's verdict to be just. If they didn't sign—so they were threatened—their other children would have to pay for it. Crying, Mrs. Schmorell said: "First, we are branded as criminals, and then we become traitors to our own children."

To Hartnagel it seemed that, "signing such a thing was more terrible than going to prison."[237]

Willi Graf, who had been tried and sentenced to death together with Alexander and Professor Huber, did not immediately follow them to the guillotine. Instead, he was subjected to continued intensive interrogation. The Gestapo was intent on extracting from him names and facts, especially in connection with his trips to various German cities in an effort to recruit collaborators from among his old comrades in the banned Catholic youth movement. Staunchly resisting the Gestapo's attempts, Willi did not betray anyone. After having spent seven months in solitary confinement, he was executed on October 12, 1943.

After the first two White Rose trials, two more years would elapse before the war ended and Hitler's regime

fell. During these two years, the Nazis continued to hunt down as many people as they could find who were in some way connected with the activities of the White Rose circle.

On the very day that Alexander and Professor Huber were executed, a third White Rose trial took place in Munich. The accused were older friends and mentors of the White Rose: the architect Manfred Eickemeyer, whose studio had been used for printing, storage, and meetings; the bookseller Josef Söhngen, who gave the students access to banned literature hidden in his store; the artist Wilhelm Geyer, whom Alexander had consulted on how to make metal stencils for the graffiti campaign; and Harald Dohrn, Christoph Probst's father-in-law, who had participated in discussions at Eickemeyer's studio. Fortunately, the exact nature and extent of the defendants' involvement with the students' resistance activities was not established, and they were sentenced to prison terms of three to six months.

A series of arrests and trials ensued in Hamburg and other cities of Germany. More people lost their lives. Among these was a chemistry student named Hans Leipelt who had gotten hold of a copy of the sixth White Rose leaflet, which he retyped and distributed in Munich and in Hamburg after the execution of the Scholls and Christoph Probst. His "crime" consisted not only of this act, but also in collecting money for the "traitor" Professor Huber's family, who were left destitute.[238]

Although Leipelt (who did not know the White Rose circle) had continued to disseminate the last White Rose leaflet in Munich, having added the boldfaced words "Despite everything, their spirit lives on!" it seemed like the Nazis's brutal and frantic efforts to suppress every manifestation of White Rose resistance had been largely successful. The student uprising that the friends had hoped for, of which the student protest of January 1943 might have been a harbinger,[239] never materialized. No more protests or demonstrations were held. No outcry on behalf of the executed students emanated from the walls of the university they had attended. On the contrary, in an assembly held shortly after the execution of Hans, Sophie, and Christoph, the students of the University of Munich applauded the custodian who had apprehended the Scholls on that fatal day in February, and greeted every mention of the students' names with shouts of condemnation.

An unexpected turn of events, however, made the voices of the White Rose heard more widely and with greater resonance than they could have envisioned. As the leaflets continued to circulate clandestinely throughout Germany, the sixth leaflet came into the hands of Count Helmuth James von Moltke, a founding member of the Kreisau Circle resistance group. Von Moltke passed it on to Bishop Eivind Berggrav in Oslo,[240] who in turn was able to have it smuggled to London via Stockholm.

In the summer of 1943, warplanes of the Royal Air Force started dropping copies of the leaflet by the millions over the cities of Germany. It was prefaced by introductory remarks regarding its authorship: "This is the text of a German leaflet of which a copy has reached England. It was written and distributed by students at the University of Munich. Six of them were executed for this, others were imprisoned." The leaflet bore a new heading, "A German leaflet—Manifesto of the Munich Students," but its wording and message were intact. It cried out for resistance to "the abominable tyrant" and his minions, "godless, arrogant, and conscienceless exploiters and executioners." A "new Europe of the spirit" must be set up. "Our people stand ready to rebel against the National Socialist enslavement of Europe in an impassioned uprising of freedom and honor."[241]

Whether reproduced clandestinely by hand within Germany, or dropped from the air by the Allies, the leaflets spread throughout the country and beyond the borders into occupied territories, making their way not only into homes, but even into concentration camps, and bringing with them hope and the consoling thought that "there were, after all, still human beings in Germany."[242]

Word of the White Rose reached the free countries, where the leaflet testified to the presence of "the other Germany."

In the summer of 1943, in an address broadcast by the BBC, the exiled German author Thomas Mann[243]

spoke of the events at the University of Munich and of the martyrdom (Mann's word) of the students and their professor, who "bear witness in the face of death that a new faith in freedom and honor is dawning.... They put their young heads on the block for their insight and for the honor of Germany.... Good, splendid young people! You shall not have died in vain; you shall not be forgotten."[244]

The *New York Times* echoed Mann's sentiments in an article entitled "Young German Martyrs," published several weeks after the execution of Alexander and Professor Huber: "These Munich students ... rose gloriously ... protesting in the name of principles which Hitler thought he had killed forever. In years to come we, too, may honor [them]."[245] Hundreds of New Yorkers flocked to Hunter College that same summer for a meeting dedicated to the memory of "six heroic victims of 'the other Germany.'" One of the speakers who paid them tribute was the First Lady Eleanor Roosevelt.[246]

Ironically, perhaps the most compelling affirmation of the moral impact of the White Rose came, as Hanser points out, from the Nazis themselves. "By the fury of their reaction," he writes, "they acknowledged that they feared the leaflets and saw them as a clear and present danger. The leaflets were bold and uncompromising expressions of the free human spirit. As such, they were an intolerable threat to the Nazi system and the concepts on which it was based and without which it could not survive."[247]

Once the Nazi regime fell, it became possible to gather and publish information about the students who had pitted themselves again the Third Reich. Their family members and White Rose survivors memorialized their deeds in books, speeches, memoirs, and interviews.[248] Streets and schools throughout Germany were named in their honor. A memorial to the White Rose was installed in the University of Munich, and the semicircular plaza in front of its central hall was renamed *Geschwister-Scholl-Platz* (Siblings Scholl Plaza). A square not far from where the Schmorell villa once stood now bears the name *Schmorell-Platz*. An annual commemoration of the White Rose takes place on February 22, the day when Hans, Sophie, and Christoph were executed. In 1987, the White Rose Foundation was founded for the purpose of preserving, studying, and disseminating information about the White Rose circle.

At the end of the war, the Gestapo files on the White Rose had been seized and taken to the Soviet Union. Later most of these documents were returned to Germany; however, those pertaining to Alexander were retained in Moscow archives, likely because Alexander had been born in Russia. It was only in 1993 that his files were brought to light and copies were sent to Munich. At last, the details of Alexander's involvement in the activities of the White Rose and his ordeal at the hands of Gestapo interrogators could be fully established.

This happened to coincide with a fortunate and providential turn of events in the history of Munich's

Russian Orthodox community. Ever since its founding in 1921, in the days when little Alexander Schmorell had attended its services with Nyanya, the parish of St Nicholas the Wonderworker had been looking to acquire or build its own place of worship. For decades, however, circumstances were unfavorable, and the parish had to rent church buildings of other religious denominations and, starting in 1960, the parish held services in a rented school building on Salvatorplatz. Pressure to vacate the premises on Salvatorplatz was mounting, but the parish had nowhere to go.

Finally, in 1993—the fiftieth anniversary of Alexander's death and the year that Alexander's files were discovered—the parish was able to purchase a church building. This church had been part of an American army base that had just been closed. It happened to be located in proximity to Stadelheim Prison, the place of Alexander's martyric death, and adjacent to the cemetery in Perlacher Forst where his earthly remains were buried. Thus, Alexander's parish is now located within a short walking distance of his final resting place. The members of that community firmly believe that this was a miracle that came about through the prayers of the martyr Alexander.

Fostered by the newly accessible material on Alexander's final struggle against the murderous Nazi regime, veneration of Alexander began to grow, especially among the youth of Orthodox Germany. More and more people began to visit Alexander's gravesite, and *panikhidas*

(memorial services) were served. When the newly purchased church was remodeled into an Orthodox place of worship,[249] Alexander was included in an icon depicting the Holy New Martyrs of Russia, albeit without a halo for the time being.

On February 4 and 5, 2012, on the feast day of the Synaxis of the Holy New Martyrs and Confessors of Russia, the glorification of St Alexander among the saints took place in the new church.[250] At these festivities, bishops and clergy of the Russian Orthodox Church Outside Russia and the Moscow Patriarchate were joined by representatives of other Orthodox Churches. This was the first glorification to be celebrated together by the two parts of the Russian Orthodox Church after the reestablishment of canonical communion.

The glorification began with a solemn procession from the cathedral to the adjacent cemetery in Perlacher Forst. At first, the procession stopped by the graves of Hans and Sophie Scholl and Christoph Probst, honoring their memory with a minute of silence. At Alexander's grave, adorned with white roses, a final panikhida was served. During the all-night vigil that followed, hymns in honor of St Alexander were chanted for the first time,[251] and his icon was brought out for veneration.[252]

St Alexander of Munich, as he is now known, is depicted on icons in white medical attire; in his hand, along with a cross, which signifies his martyrdom, he holds a white rose. The day of his commemoration is on

the day of his martyric death, July 13 (n.s.), the Synaxis of the Holy Apostles.

In a sermon during the glorification festivities, Metropolitan Onufry of Chernovtsy noted, "Service to Christ takes different forms and modes in accordance with times and circumstances."[253] It has been noted that St Alexander's courageous spiritual exploit is akin to that of other Orthodox, such as the New Martyrs of Russia, who suffered at the hands of godless authorities in the unprecedented, monstrously brutal persecutions of the twentieth century. The violence of these persecutions has an inner logic that was perceived by Solzhenitsyn: "Let us not forget that violence does not live alone and is not capable of living alone: it is necessarily interwoven with falsehood. Between them lies the most intimate, the deepest of natural bonds. Violence finds its only refuge in falsehood, falsehood its only support in violence."[254]

Serving Their Deepest Convictions and the Truth

St Alexander, his friends, and mentors opposed National Socialism primarily from the standpoint of their Christian faith. They perceived Nazi ideology as an assault on Truth. In the ambition of the Nazi creed to destroy the existing order of society, in its fierce determination to annihilate Jews, Slavs, Gypsies, and all whom it deemed unworthy of existence, the White Rose saw an assault on the very concept of Man who was created in God's image. It was an assault on God himself.

The authors of the White Rose leaflets, Alexander and Hans, ascribe a spiritual significance to their resistance to Nazism, which they call "the dictatorship of evil."[255] In their fourth leaflet, they present this resistance as a struggle against "the National Socialist terrorist state ... the struggle against the devil, against the servants

of Antichrist." It is of utmost importance, they continue, to realize that

> everywhere and at all times, demons have been lurking in the dark, waiting for the moment when man is weak; when of his own volition he leaves his place in the order of Creation as founded for him by God in freedom; when he yields to the force of evil, separates himself from the powers of a higher order and, after voluntarily taking the first step, is driven on to the next and the next at a furiously accelerating pace.

One must therefore cling to God, as "of course man is free, but without God he is defenseless against evil. He is like a rudderless ship, at the mercy of the storm, an infant without his mother, a cloud dissolving into thin air."

The accuracy of the young people's perception of the fundamental antagonism of National Socialism to Christianity was corroborated by the Nazis themselves (although, like the Communists in Russia, they made efforts to disguise and deny this). In a secret circular of June 9, 1941, Martin Bormann, Hitler's second in command, divulged the fact that the repressive measures against the Churches of Germany were aimed against Christianity itself. The circular opened with the following words: "National Socialism and Christianity are irreconcilable."[256] In a private conversation, the head of the dreaded SS, Heinrich

Himmler, boasted that "We shall not rest until we have rooted out Christianity."[257]

Roland Freisler, the judge who presided at the first two trials of the White Rose, was of one mind with Himmler and Bormann. His antipathy to Christianity came out most explicitly during the trial of the Kreisau Circle. Helmuth von Moltke, who was tried as one of the founders of the circle, described the trial in a letter, smuggled out by the prison chaplain, to his wife:

> I stood there as a Christian and as nothing else … Freisler was the only one of the whole gang [of Nazi functionaries present at the trial] who thoroughly understood me, and the only one of them who realized why he must do away with me … "From whom do you take your orders, from the other world or from Adolf Hitler? Where lie your loyalty and your faith?" Rhetorical questions of course. . . . The decisive phrase in the proceedings, which Freisler said to me in the course of one of his tirades, was: "Herr Graf, Christianity has one thing in common with us National Socialists, and one thing only: we claim the whole man."[258]

These sentiments did not come out with such clarity and force during the White Rose trials. However, it is reasonable to conclude that, in the demonic fury that Freisler unleashed at the students, he was driven at least in part by his hatred for Christianity, especially if the expression of their Christian beliefs during interrogations and the

explicitly Christian passages of the White Rose leaflets are taken into account.

In a diary entry from 1940, Theodor Haecker, one of the White Rose mentors, reflected thus on the Nazis: "Their attitude to the Christian religion is not simply machiavellian, or napoleonic, or fascist, a purely political attitude, bent upon bringing Christianity under their dominion; no, they mean to destroy and supplant it. Salus ex Germanis: A German saviour and bearer of light is to replace Christ."[259] Many Christian believers and clergy among the Germans who shared Haecker's insight did not doubt that the military victory of National Socialism would lead to unbridled persecution of the Christian religion in Germany. Nazi treatment of Christians in occupied territories likewise did not bode well, in the event of a Nazi victory, for Christianity beyond the borders of Germany.[260]

The underlying rationale of the Nazi agenda to eradicate Christianity was clearly stated in a lecture for Nazi youth leaders: "National Socialism is a religion, born out of blood and race, not a political world view. It is the new, only true religion, born out of a Nordic spirit and an Arian soul. The religions still existing must disappear as soon as possible. If they do not dissolve themselves the State must destroy them."[261] Hitler put it succinctly: "We, too, are the Church. Its day has gone."[262]

Thus it would be a mistake to view the White Rose and its activities as sheer political activism. Time and again, both the main actors in the White Rose drama and those who wrote reminiscences about them stressed that theirs was not a circle of politically minded individuals who gathered to discuss political agendas. Sophie Scholl expressed it thus: "Although I don't know much about politics and have no ambition to do so, I do have some idea of right and wrong, because that has nothing to do with politics."[263]

Lilo Ramdohr remembers that, even though Alexander was a vigorous opponent of both Bolshevism and National Socialism, "never did I have the impression that his main interest lay in politics. Instead it lay in a love for everything that was true and beautiful, and in the realization of this love in the world."[264] Even in the political declaration that he was required to write during his interrogations, Alexander did not present himself as a proponent of any one political system:

> If you asked me which form of government I prefer, I would have to answer: That form which corresponds best to the character of the country in question. . . . Hence, I am by no means a resolute advocate of monarchy, democracy, socialism or whatever all the various forms may be called. What is good for one country, or possibly even the best, may perhaps be the worst for another, something quite unsuitable for it.[265]

At a memorial gathering in 1946, Christoph Probst's sister Angelika portrayed him thus:

> Christoph is not to be characterized by the words "revolutionary" or "freedom fighter." He was fundamentally not a political person.[266] He only seemed to be one, as everything that contradicted his way of thinking and living was most concentratedly embodied in those who were politically in power. Thus his fight against them bore much more of a religious than a political character.[267]

The White Rose was a circle of friends—young people who gathered, sometimes with older mentors, for evenings of reading and conversation. Literature, theology, and history were discussed "without any concrete objectives," wrote Traute Lafrenz in her reminiscences. "Only at the end did we discuss, briefly at most, the political situation, the inescapable hopelessness with which everything was drifting blindly towards ruin."[268] For Josef Söhngen, the bookseller who had provided his young friends with banned books, it was indisputable that their actions were rooted in an "explicit and clearly-articulated religious worldview."[269]

Among the favorite reading of some of the White Rose students (especially Sophie Scholl) were the works of St Augustine. Perhaps passages from his writings, such as the following, influenced their convictions. Commenting on a passage from the Prophet

Ezekiel that speaks of those who love God,[270] Augustine writes: "Though they did not correct the sins which were 'done in the midst of them,' yet they sorrowed for them, and by that very sorrow separated themselves; ... How great security is granted to you, my brethren, who among this people are sighing and moaning for the iniquities which are being done in the midst of you, and who do them not!"[271] Or perhaps it is we—reading this passage now, many years after the students' execution—who can see how vividly it applies to them.

Although the young people could not "correct the sins which were done in the midst of them," their "sighing and moaning" included a call to their countrymen to abandon their apathy. As they wrote in their fourth leaflet, "Everywhere and at all times of greatest trial men have appeared, prophets and saints who cherished their freedom, who preached the One God and who with His help brought the people to a reversal of their downward course." It is imperative, they assert, to follow the example of these people, to arouse oneself from lethargy, and to summon the strength to shake off the "cloak of indifference," the apathy which allows evil men to act as they do. It is one's moral duty to do so. "Has not God given you the strength and will to fight?" Anyone who does not feel compassion for the numberless victims of the bloody regime, who does not protest but tolerates, is in fact himself guilty.[272]

The state of apathy, the habit of indifference, is one that several fathers of the Church warn against as a most serious sin. St John Chrysostom, in his *Homilies on Genesis*, places indifference at the root of the Fall, and envisions God addressing Adam with the following words: "So what kind of terrible indifference (*rhathymia*) is this that, despite your having such great enjoyment, you could not bear to keep away from that one thing but rather hastened in that manner to violate the command given you by me and envelop yourself in so many excesses?"[273]

As Solzhenitsyn observes, apathetic passivity is a form of complicity: "[Violence] does not always, not necessarily, openly throttle the throat, more often it demands from its subjects only an oath of allegiance to falsehood, only complicity in falsehood. And the simple step of a simple courageous man is not to partake in falsehood, not to support false actions!"[274]

Metropolitan Onufry likened St Alexander's denunciation of National Socialism (expressed both in the White Rose leaflets and in his interrogations) to the daring feat of St John the Baptist, who had denounced the king, Herod, for unlawfully marrying his brother's wife Herodias. Beheading was the retribution he suffered for his audacious words.

Compelled by their Christian consciences to act—to denounce and oppose the tyranny of Hitler's regime—Alexander and his friends set themselves the task of

"calling out the truth as clearly and audibly as possible into the German night."[275] In unmasking the excesses and true nature of the regime, they boldly ventured on a course of action that they knew would put them in mortal danger. They were standing up not to a fatally wounded evil, but to an evil still quite alive. It was their Christian faith that gave them the fortitude to willingly risk their lives, to sacrifice themselves for others and for the sake of serving their "deepest convictions and the truth."[276]

A Saint for Our Time

One of the people who knew Alexander best, Ange-lika Probst, remarked after his death that, in the letters he had written to his family from prison, she did not recognize the lively and life-loving Alexander she had known. The letters, she said, were "not characteristic of him."[277] Perhaps this may be ascribed to the fact that there had always been a side of him—his inner spiritual life—that he had not been in the habit of divulging, even to those who were close to him. Yet the many months that St Alexander spent in prison awaiting his execution must surely have effected a certain transformation in him. His letters from prison testify to his final struggle, in which he used his persecution as an occasion to attain blessed-ness. Having cleansed himself of his passions through sor-row and suffering, having "put off the old man with his

deeds, and [having] put on the new man who is renewed in knowledge,"[278] he came to express the following convictions:

"Death" does not mean the end of all life, but actually, on the contrary, a birth, a passing over into a new life, a glorious and everlasting life. Hence death is not a fearful thing. (Letter of May 30)

This whole terrible "misfortune" has been necessary to show me the right way—and therefore it has actually not been a misfortune at all. Above all, I am glad, and grateful to God for it, that it has been granted to me to understand this sign from Him, and thereby to find the right way. For what did I know before this of faith, of true, deep faith, of truth, of the ultimate and only truth of God? Very little! But now I have progressed so far that I am happy and calm and confident even in my present situation—come what may. (Letter of July 2)

God arranges everything according to His will, and for our good. We must simply always place ourselves trustingly in His hands, and then He will never forsake us, but will always help and console us. (Letter of June 5)

These words are indicative of a state such as St Isaac the Syrian describes:

For God's protection and providence encircle all men, yet they are not seen except by those who have cleansed themselves from sin and who continually keep their attention on God,

and on Him alone. But God's providence is especially apparent to them when they enter into a great trial on behalf of the
Truth; for then they perceive it as if seeing it with their bodily
eyes.[279]

And so, having endured his "trial on behalf of truth"
and being sure of God's providence, Alexander passed
into a new life and thus into eternal glory in Christ. The
rite of glorification that took place in Munich was not
performed for his benefit, but for ours. Furthermore, "it
is not we who have glorified Alexander," remarked Metropolitan Onufry. "God glorified him! We have only proclaimed his name." Glorification is not an act that sets a
seal of approval or commendation upon a person. Rather
it opens up the way for those who are still living on earth
to address in prayer someone who is already in the presence of God's everlasting glory.

Thus, the glorification of St Alexander has given us the
opportunity for the most immediate kind of communion
with him, which no amount of reading or research will
give us—that is, prayerful communion. We can address
him both in collective prayer, during a service on the day
of his memory, and in private.

In St Alexander, who was always so perceptive and
responsive to the needs of others,[280] we have acquired
a prayerful intercessor whose own life may make him
inclined to be sympathetic to the prayerful pleas we
address to him in various situations:

—as a medic, to answer our prayers for health;

—as a person of warmhearted generosity and profound compassion, to aid us when we are experiencing want or misfortune;

—as one who encountered a prolonged period of pressing disquiet and anxiety, to console us in our bleak moments;

—as a student, to help youth in their academic endeavors and career choices;

—as a young man, to respond sympathetically to the predicaments and emotional upheavals of young people;

—as one who came from a family of mixed national and religious heritage, to lend a hand in the struggle of those who seek to strike a balance between different worlds;

—as an Orthodox person who lived among non-Orthodox in a Western country, to strengthen us in our Orthodox faith; and

—as one who faced an ever-increasing onslaught of iniquity, to send us discernment and moral fortitude.

Metropolitan Onufry reminds us that "if, during the course of our life, it falls to our lot to uphold Truth and Goodness, we must pray to St Alexander, and he will strengthen us."

St Alexander can now be, as Metropolitan Hilarion, first hierarch of the Russian Orthodox Church Outside

Russia, pointed out, "an intercessor of our spiritual correction, of the renewal of our lives and our inner strength!"[281]

A saint, however, is not only a prayerful intercessor but also a model, an example for us to follow. What does this young man—who was neither a wise elder, nor an ascetic, nor an eloquent theologian—have to offer us by way of example or instruction? The narrative of St Alexander's life reminds us to be judicious in our choice of friends and in the heroes we hold up as models for our children and ourselves.

We may seek inspiration in his steadfast devotion—to Truth, to his cause, to his friends. Remembering him, we may be infected with his radiant joy of life, remembering also to thank God for all the blessings, and even the sorrows, He sends our way.

We might emulate St Alexander in his inclination to seek out and appreciate beauty, whether this beauty be found in nature or in literature, music, and art. For in the beauty of nature we may apprehend the Creator from his creation. As for the arts—exposure to the finest specimens of human creative expression can act as a counterforce to what Fr Seraphim (Rose) calls "the emotional and spiritual wasteland of our times," by enriching and refining our souls.[282]

St Alexander's example reminds us that right differs from wrong; that in our dealings with the world surrounding us, we must always be guided by our conscience; and that faith cannot be subdued by violence.

He teaches us to hope that even in the midst of suffering and affliction, if we endure patiently, with trust in God's providence, we can find solace and even joy.

If, like St Alexander, we realize that "here we have no continuing city, but seek the one to come,"[283] if we strive to know and love God, and to keep His commandments, then the grace that He bestows upon us in return will join with our feeble efforts and help us to transcend our limitations. The story of Alexander's life and death clearly demonstrates that this is indeed the way we attain salvation, and that in this manner even ordinary, normal people can—nay, are called to—become saints.[284]

"It is God's providence that dictates *when* a saint's name is revealed to mankind," observed Metropolitan Onufry. St Alexander's recent glorification may be seen as an indication that God, in his solicitous care for us, has revealed St Alexander specifically as a saint for our time.

Let us hold dear the memory of St Alexander, praying to him to "intercede with God for our solace and peace" (as he promised his loved ones in his final letter), and treasuring the counsel that he has entrusted to our hearts: "Do not forget God!"

The Life of St Anthimus of Nicomedia (September 3/16)

The life of St Anthimus, on whose day St Alexander was born, contains several remarkable parallels to the narrative of the latter's martyric death and to the story of the White Rose.

St Anthimus, bishop of Nicomedia, was martyred during the last and fiercest persecution of Christians in the Roman Empire, referred to sometimes as "The Great Persecution" (303–311). This persecution was unleashed and carried out by the emperor Diocletian at the instigation of Galerius, his assistant and designated successor, and with the consent of his co-emperor, Maximian. Diocletian had made Nicomedia the capital of his (eastern) portion of the Roman Empire, while Maximian ruled the western portion from Milan.

Nicomedia had a sizeable Christian population. Even members of the imperial household, including

Diocletian's wife, Prisca, and their daughter, Valeria, were Christians. A Christian basilica had been built on high ground, and was visible from the palace. On February 23, 303, Diocletian ordered that the church be demolished, its books burned, and its treasures confiscated. On the following day, February 24, he issued an edict ordering the destruction of all Christian church buildings within the empire and the burning of all Christian Scripture and liturgical books and forbidding Christians to gather for worship. A Christian citizen of Nicomedia tore down the edict from the wall upon which it had been prominently displayed, ripped it to pieces, and loudly denounced the emperor for his injustice and the pagans for their iniquity. He was seized and martyred. Many Christians who resisted the edict were subjected to torture and death.

A fire broke out in the imperial palace. The Christians were accused of having set it as revenge for the destruction of their churches and writings. Some believed, however, that the emperor was responsible for the fire, which he used as a pretext for the intensification of persecutions. Stricter edicts followed, decreeing that bishops, priests, and deacons be arrested and imprisoned and compelled by torture to perform pagan sacrifice. By early 304, the Christian laity were required to sacrifice to the gods and the empire upon pain of death. These edicts were enforced with ferocious cruelty, and Christians were martyred in countless numbers, sometimes in large groups at

one time. The persecutions continued unabated until the year 311.

Among the first Nicomedian Christians to suffer for their faith during the Great Persecution were highly placed members of the imperial court. Diocletian's Grand Chamberlain Dorotheus and several others—Gorgonius, Peter, Migdonius, Mardonius, and Indis—were cast into prison, where they suffered various tortures and finally executed. The bodies of Gorgonius, Indis, and Peter were thrown into the sea, but miraculously recovered. The virgin Domna, a Christian who had been a pagan priestess associated with the court, gave honorable burial to the relics of these three martyrs and was beheaded for doing so.

The bishop of Nicomedia, Anthimus, had gone into hiding at the insistence of his flock. From there, he wrote letters that he sent secretly to the imprisoned members of the royal household and to other suffering Christians in his spiritual charge. He exhorted them to bear their affliction with joy at the thought of dying for Christ. One of these letters was intercepted, and its bearer, Deacon Theophilus, refusing to reveal the whereabouts of Bishop Anthimus, was tortured and executed.

A detachment of soldiers was sent to search for St Anthimus and encountered him but did not recognize him. Anthimus invited the soldiers to partake of a meal that he prepared for them, and then revealed his identity. The soldiers, moved by the saint's heartfelt hospitality, were at a loss as to what they should do. They considered

returning empty-handed and saying that they had not found Bishop Anthimus. However, he could not condone the sin of lying and insisted that the soldiers lead him back to Nicomedia.

The emperor had St Anthimus bound and then ordered that instruments of torture be brought in, thinking that this would unnerve the bishop and force him to submit to the emperor's will. Anthimus fearlessly faced the emperor, saying: "I welcome your threats of torture and execution, as they would only liberate me from the bonds of my flesh and transport me to the realm for which I pine with my entire being." Thereupon the tyrant ordered Anthimus to be tortured in various ways, imprisoned, and then beheaded. Upon reaching the place of execution, the bishop asked to be allowed to pray. Then, bowing his head, he peacefully and joyfully submitted to the executioner's sword. At nightfall, several of the faithful came to the place of execution and carried away the remains of the saint, giving them a proper and noble burial.

The lives of the three tyrants—Diocletian, Galerius, and Maximian—came to ignoble ends. Galerius suffered an especially awful sickness and committed suicide, as did Maximian, and, likely, Diocletian.

* * *

Significantly, February 23 (some sources give the date as February 24) was the festival of the god Terminus,

Roman God of boundaries and frontiers, who was thought to reside in and protect markers delineating the borders of properties. In the center of Rome, a small shrine within the Temple of Jupiter dedicated to Terminus, whose presence there safeguarded the power of Rome and its boundaries. Diocletian's choice of February 23 as the beginning of his persecution of Christians has been construed as his attempt to enlist the aid of Terminus in limiting or terminating Christianity.

It is interesting to note that February 24 was a significant date for the Nazis—it was the day in 1920 that the National Socialist Party had been founded and was marked yearly as a special occasion.

The first cluster of reprisals against the White Rose circle occurred around February 24. The hurried show trial and execution of Hans, Sophie and Christoph took place on February 22; they were buried on February 24. It was on the 24th that the Nazis published wanted notices and posters with Alexander's photo. Alexander was identified and arrested that very evening.

It is almost as if, in the year 1943, the Nazis were echoing their spiritual forerunners, the impious pagan emperors of the year 303, in their brutal quest to eliminate steadfast and noble Christians who were in opposition to their iniquitous rule.

Alexander's Description of the Paschal Service in 1941

(Excerpted from a letter to Angelika Knoop)

> *In 1941, the parish of St Nicholas was holding services in a rented hall at 5 Mathildenstrasse. That year, parish warden Sophia Durnovo filed a written request with the Munich police, asking for permission to hold the services of Holy Week and Pascha from April 12 until April 20. She added that the parish was anticipating about 250 people attending, consisting of Russian and Bulgarian faithful. The authorities allowed the services, but forbade holding the traditional Easter procession and service at midnight.*[285]

Munich, April 20, 1941

Morning

Today is Russian Easter. Once more, a kulich[286] stands on the table. . . . I've attended church services more often

lately, and today I'll go again. Today, of course, is the greatest church feast. Properly, it should be celebrated at midnight, but these days this sort of thing is forbidden. So we will have the service in the morning.

Evening

Let me tell you what it was like in church. The cold, plain hall was so beautifully decorated, it had become so warm through the love with which it had been festively adorned. Above, on the wooden beams—two meters high—lay fresh evergreen branches. Among these stood small saucers with wax lights. Everything was decorated with flowers, all the images were framed by them, all the crosses received a mantle of evergreen. And there were so many candles blazing!

The hall gradually filled with people and, as the service began, each person lit the candle that he held in his hand; everyone had a light. That was very beautiful—this warm candlelight flooding everything; it was a luminous sea of light.

And then you heard the bass voice of the priest, who was fully vested in gold-embroidered vestments, and the sound of the choir singing the glorious Russian church hymns, which on Easter are especially beautiful. And everything took place so solemnly and slowly. Once in a while, though, when the joy became overly great, the basses in the choir boomed, just barely kept in check by the beat. . . .

The priest, with three candles in his hand, came out again and again and exclaimed to the people: "Christ is risen!" And each time everyone answered in unison: "Truly He is risen!" This, you see, is the Easter greeting. At the end of the service, everyone filed by the priest, kissing him on the cheeks three times. And then began the general Easter greeting, when each person whom one holds dear or respects received three kisses on the cheek.

All this lasted 3 1/2 hours, so you can imagine how festively everything was conducted.

Chronology

1917 **September 16:** Alexander Schmorell born in Orenburg, Russia.

1918 Alexander's mother dies.

1920 Hugo Schmorell remarries.

1921 The Schmorell family leaves Russia and settles in Munich, Germany. Alexander's nanny accompanies the family into exile.

1921 The parish of St Nicholas is founded in Munich.

1933 Hitler assumes dictatorial powers in Germany.

1935 Alexander and Christoph Probst meet at the Neue Realgymnasium where both are students and become close friends.

1936   Alexander passes his Abitur.
Serves six months in the Reichsarbeitsdienst.
Begins compulsory military service.

1938   Alexander's unit takes part in the annexation of Austria and the occupation of the Sudetenland.

1939   **Spring:** Alexander released from military service.
Begins to study medicine.
September: German troops invade Poland.
World War II begins.
Fall: Alexander meets Nikolai Hamazaspian.

1940   **Spring:** Alexander conscripted, sent with a medical unit to France.
Fall: Alexander returns to Munich and to his study of medicine.
Meets Hans Scholl who is also a medical student at the University of Munich.

1941   **April:** Alexander assigned to the Second Student-Military Company.
June 22: Germany declares war on Russia.
September: Alexander meets Lilo Ramdohr at an art studio where both are taking a class.

1942   **May:** Sophie Scholl begins her studies in Munich.
June/July: The first four White Rose leaflets are written and distributed.
July: Hans and Alexander meet Willi Graf in the Second Student-Military Company.
July 23: Alexander, Hans, and Willi leave for the Russian front.
November: The student medics return from Russia.
Alexander and Hans meet Falk Harnack through Lilo Ramdohr.

1943   **January 13:** Gauleiter Giesler's speech at the University of Munich anniversary gathering causes an outbreak of student protest.
Mid-January: The fifth leaflet is written and widely disseminated.
February 2: The Sixth German army capitulates at Stalingrad.
February 3, 8, and 15: During the night, Hans, Alexander, and Willi paint anti-Nazi graffiti on the walls of Munich buildings.
Mid-February: Professor Huber writes the sixth leaflet.
February 18: Hans and Sophie Scholl are arrested after distributing leaflets at the university.
Willi Graf is arrested on the same evening.
February 19: Alexander flees Munich late at night.

February 20: Christoph Probst arrested in Innsbruck.

February 22: Hans, Sophie, and Christoph are tried by the People's Court and sentenced to death. Late that same afternoon, they are executed by guillotine.

February 24: Alexander's photo is published as a wanted person. Alexander returns to Munich late at night, where he is identified and arrested. Earlier that day, Hans, Sophie, and Christoph are buried in the cemetery at Perlacher Forst.

February 25, 26, March 1, 11, 13, 18: Interrogations of Alexander Schmorell.

February 26: Alexander's parents and siblings are taken into clan custody.

March 20: Alexander's family is released from prison.

April 15: Alexander's parents are arrested again; they remain in prison for three weeks.

April 19: Great and Holy Monday. Alexander, Willi, and Professor Huber are tried by the People's Court and sentenced to death. Eleven others are tried the same day, but receive lighter sentences.

April 25: Western Easter and Orthodox Pascha coincide.

July 13: Alexander and Professor Huber are executed.

July 14: Alexander is buried in the cemetery at Perlacher Forst.

October 12: Willi Graf is executed.

1945   **May:** Germany surrenders.

1993   Fifty years after his death, files pertaining to Alexander Schmorell (including interrogations transcripts) are discovered in Moscow archives and copies are sent to Munich.

The parish of St Nicholas acquires its own church building adjacent to Perlacher Forst, where Alexander is buried.

2012   **February 5:** Glorification among the saints of St Alexander.

ACKNOWLEDGMENTS

I wish to express my gratitude to Priest Michael van Opstall, Irene Hanlon, Michael Perekrestov, Elizabeth Purdy, and Isaac Williams for reading the manuscript of this book; their editorial suggestions and insightful comments resulted in significant improvement. Thanks are also due to Hieromonk Alexander (Reichert) whose advice and never-failing help I have enjoyed in translating troublesome passages from the German. I owe a special debt of gratitude to Ksenia Golenovsky Bogolubov for sharing her reminiscences of Alexander Schmorell; and to Helen Bogolubov Desai for eliciting, recording, and communicating to me her mother's recollections. With thanks I would like to acknowledge the kindly help of Eugenia Urtiew and Paul Urtiew who gladly related their fond memories of Bishop Alexander (Lovchii), provided me

with his photograph along with a copy of one of his Sunday bulletins, and answered numerous questions about Russian émigré life in Munich of the 1940s. Invaluable assistance has come from Archpriest Nikolai Artemoff of Munich, who generously furnished me with books, articles, reminiscences, and photos in response to my repeated queries. I have benefited from the advice and aid of Katja Yurschak and Lettie Savage in the final stages of this book's preparation. To the staff of Holy Trinity Publications, I extend my deepest gratitude for all their patient and diligent help.

Without the advice and support of my loved ones and friends, who were a constant source of encouragement and prayers, I would not have been able to complete my work. To them I extend my affectionate and heartfelt thanks.

—EP

NOTES

Chapter 1

1. Alexander Solzhenitsyn, "Nobel Lecture in Literature (1970)." *Nobelprize.org.* http://www.nobelprize.org/nobel_prizes/literature/laureates/1970/solzhenitsyn-lecture.html

2. Rom 5:20.

3. Lilo Ramdohr, as quoted in Lucy Burns, "White Rose: The Germans Who Tried to Topple Hitler," *BBC Magazine*, February 22, 2013, http://www.bbc.co.uk/news/magazine-21521060. Still alive when the glorification took place, Lilo Ramdohr passed away about a year later (in May 2013) at the age of ninety-nine.

4. Richard Hanser, *A Noble Treason: The Revolt of the Munich Students against Hitler* (San Francisco: Ignatius Press, 2012), 23.

5. Elisabeth Brinkmann, *Der Letzte Gang: Ein Priesterleben Im Dienste Todgeweihter: Erinnerungen an Meinen Bruder* (Münster, Westfalen: Aschendorff, 1950), 40.

6. Examples would include people who refused to join the Nazi party or the Hitler Youth despite pressure to do so and various negative consequences of their refusal. Also, those who sheltered Jews, shopkeepers who continued to serve their Jewish customers, schoolmasters and -mistresses

who took in Jewish children, although all this was forbidden and punishable as a crime.

7. John S. Conway, *The Nazi Persecution of the Churches 1933–45* (New York: Basic Books, 1968), xiv.

8. Ibid., 2.

9. Ibid., 15.

10. Ibid., 148.

11. Ibid., 155.

12. Niemöller later suffered incarceration at Dachau; Bonhoeffer was executed in April 1945.

13. Hans Rothfels, *The German Opposition to Hitler: An Assessment* (London: G. Wolff, 1970), 112. Interestingly, von Moltke wrote this at a time when German success in the war still seemed possible—and even likely—to most Germans.

14. Daniel Horn, "Youth Resistance in the Third Reich: A Social Portrait," *Journal of Social History*, 7, no. 1 (1973): 26–50.

15. From the first leaflet of the White Rose.

16. Sophie Scholl—21, Christoph Probst—23 (father of three small children), Hans Scholl and Willi Graf—24, Alexander Schmorell—25, Professor Kurt Huber—49.

17. The story of the White Rose is the subject of the film *Sophie Scholl: The Final Days* [in German with English subtitles], Dir. Marc Rothemund (2005).

Chapter 2

18. September 3 according to the Julian Calendar, which was used in Russia before the revolution and is still used by the Russian Orthodox Church in the twenty-first century. On September 3/16 we celebrate the memory of St Anthimus of Nicomedia, whose life contains many startling parallels to the life of St Alexander. See Appendix 1 for a short life of St Anthimus.

19. The facts of St Alexander's early life are compiled from: Igor Khramov, *Russkaia Dusha Beloi Rozy* [The Russian Soul of the White Rose] (Orenburg: Usadba, 2009) and from the biographical introduction to the collected letters of Alexander Schmorell and Christoph Probst in Alexander Schmorell, Christoph Probst, and Christiane Moll, *Alexander*

Schmorell, Christoph Probst: Gesammelte Briefe (Berlin: Lukas Verlag, 2011), hereafter cited as *Briefe*.

20. While some sources, including family reminiscences, state that Natalia Vvedenskaia was the daughter of a priest, Khramov writes that she was the daughter of a civil servant (Khramov, *Russkaia Dusha*).

21. Feodosia Lapschina (1877–1960) outlived Alexander by seventeen years and was buried in the cemetery of Perlacher Forst not far from him, under the name of Franziska Schmorell. A later headstone—erected after Erich Schmorell, brother of Alexander, was interred in the same grave— gives her name merely as "Njanja" (Find A Grave Memorial, #73654445).

22. As a result of the combined efforts of his nanny and stepmother, Alexander's religious upbringing was more intensive than that which other members of his family received.

23. Ksenia Golenovsky Bogolubov, oral reminiscences of Alexander Schmorell, as recorded and communicated to the author by Helen Bogolubov Desai, May 9, 2015. The Lenten diet would omit all meat and dairy products.

24. Alexander Schmorell, letter to Angelika Knoop, May 30, 1942, *Briefe*, 472. (Translations of German texts are my own, unless otherwise noted. —*EP*)

25. Leonid Pasternak's son, poet and novelist Boris Pasternak, who had remained in Russia, would write *Doctor Zhivago* years later.

26. Ksenia Golenovsky Bogolubov, oral reminiscences of Alexander Schmorell.

27. Reminiscences of Maria T., as communicated to the author by Archpriest Nikolai Artemoff in an e-mail on November 24, 2015.

28. Alexander Schmorell, letter to Valia, November 25, 1942, *Briefe*, 511.

29. *Abitur*—final exams at the end of secondary education enabling one to enter university.

30. Prior to the Nazi takeover, German schools offered religious instruction in either the Catholic or the Protestant faith, according to a student's preference.

31. Karlheinz Niedermayr as quoted in *Briefe,* 42.

Chapter 3

32. Christoph's father was a scholar of Asian culture with an interest in Eastern religions. After his divorce from Christoph's mother, he had married a Jewish woman.

33. Erich Schmorell as quoted in *Briefe*, 82.

34. Christoph Probst, letter to Elise Probst, June 24, 1936, *Briefe*, 86.

35. Angelika Probst as quoted in *Briefe*, 82.

36. Traute Lafrenz as quoted in *Briefe*, 101.

37. Rose Nägele as quoted in *Briefe*, 510, n. 582.

38. Inge Scholl and Dorothee Sölle, *The White Rose: Munich, 1942–1943* (Hanover, NH: Wesleyan University Press, 1983), 21. Hereafter, this work by Scholl and Sölle (along with Khramov's biography and Moll's introduction to *Briefe*) will furnish material for our narrative, along with two additional sources: Hanser, *Noble Treason* (cited in chapter 1, note 4) and Annette Dumbach and Jud Newborn, *Sophie Scholl and the White Rose* (London: Oneworld Publications, 2006).

39. Alexander Schmorell, letter to Angelika Knoop, April 19, 1941. *Briefe*, 348.

40. Alexander Schmorell, letter to Angelika Probst, May 1, 1937, *Briefe,* 295.

41. This was not the Soviet Union of Stalin, but rather a somewhat idealized Russia that hearkened back to prerevolutionary times.

42. Scholl and Sölle, *The White Rose*, 16.

43. Dumbach and Newborn, *Sophie Scholl*, 53.

44. Alexander Schmorell, letter to Angelika Knoop, June 26, 1941, *Briefe*, 428.

45. Lilo Ramdohr, *Freundschaften in Der Weißen Rose* (München: Verl. Geschichtswerkstatt Neuhausen, 1995), 24. Hereafter cited as *Freundschaften*.

46. Hans Scholl, diary entry for August 9, 1942, in Hans Scholl, Inge Jens, Sophie Scholl, John Brownjohn (trans.), and Richard Gilman, *At the Heart of the White Rose: Letters and Diaries of Hans and Sophie Scholl* (New York: Harper & Row, 1987), 224; hereafter cited as *Letters and Diaries*.

47. Hans had been forbidden to read a favorite book by Stefan Zweig on the grounds that the author was Jewish, and, on another occasion, was threatened with punishment for singing Norwegian and Russian folk songs around the campfire.

48. Abbreviation for *Deutsche Jungenschaft, November 1* (the date in 1929 of the group's founding).

49. Hans Scholl, letter to Inge Scholl, August 1, 1940, *Letters and Diaries*, 56.

50. Hans Scholl, diary entry for July 31, 1942, *Letters and Diaries*, 223.

51. Alexander Schmorell, letter to Angelika Knoop, April 14, 1941, *Briefe*, 340.

52. Ibid.

53. Nikolai Nikolaeff-Hamazaspian (1920–2013) came from an Armenian family that had lived in Russia for several generations. After the Russian Revolution, the family emigrated to Bulgaria. Nikolai came to study in Munich, where he met Alexander and became good friends with him, spending much time reading and discussing the works of Dostoyevsky together.

54. Interview with Nikolai Hamazaspian as quoted in Ulrich Chaussy and Gerd R. Ueberschär, *"Es Lebe Die Freiheit!": Die Geschichte Der Weißen Rose Und Ihrer Mitglieder in Dokumenten Und Berichten* (Frankfurt am Main: Fischer Taschenbuch, 2013), 124.

55. According to an eyewitness, Russian émigrés, heeding the appeal of their pastors, would linger around Russian prisoner-of-war (POW) camps for days on end, waiting for an opportunity to pass on to the inmates something they had brought for them. M. V. Shkarovskii, *Krest i Svastika: Natsistskaia Germaniia i Pravoslavnaia Tserkov'* (Moskva: Veche, 2007), 23. In her reminiscences, Ksenia Golenovsky Bogolubov recalls accompanying Alexander on a humanitarian undertaking. They would board a train that went through fields where Russian POWs were performing forced labor under the watchful eye of armed guards and would throw the Russians food and cigarettes.

Chapter 4

56. Harald Dohrn was shot by the *Schutzstaffel* (SS) in Munich, just hours before American tanks rolled into the city, for his involvement in the anti-Nazi uprising *Freiheitsaktion Bayern* (Bavarian Freedom Action) in April 1945. The aim of the uprising was to topple the Nazis from power in Bavaria and to prevent unnecessary destruction and bloodshed in resistance to the advancing U.S. army. Although the Nazis captured and executed the insurgents, several Bavarian towns heeded the call and surrendered peacefully to the Allies; thus lives were saved.

57. Christoph Probst as quoted in Scholl and Sölle, *The White Rose*, 37.

58. Willi's main contribution to the work of the friends took place during the second phase of their activities—after their return from Russia in the fall of 1942.

59. Interestingly, Willi noted in his diary on November 19, 1942, that he was reading Nikolai Gogol's *Meditations on the Divine Liturgy*, which he found to be "valuable." Willi Graf, Anneliese Knoop-Graf, and Inge Jens, *Briefe Und Aufzeichnungen* (Frankfurt am Main: Fischer Taschenbuch, 2004), 79. The latest of several German translations of Gogol's work had been published in 1938.

60. Willi Graf as quoted in Hanser, *Noble Treason*, 140.

61. Ibid., 155.

62. Ibid., 142.

63. *Freundschaften*, 29.

64. Alexander's stepmother kept his prayer book to the end of her days, asking to be buried with it. *O zhyzni I podvige novomuchenika Aleksandra Miunkhenskogo, Schmorelia* [On the Life and Podvig of New martyr Alexander Schmorell of Munich]: http://www.sobor.de/index. php?option=com_content&view=article&id=198%3Aueber-das-leben-und-den-einsatz-von-alexander-schmorell&catid=79%3Aalexander-sch-morell-verherrlichung&Itemid=109&lang=ru

65. Audio interview with Lilo Ramdohr on BBC World Service *Witness*, February 23, 2013, http://www.bbc.co.uk/programmes/p014knxl.

66. Reminiscence of Margaret Knittel as quoted in *Briefe*, 522 n. 614.

67. Inge Scholl portrays Sophie as deducing that Hans had authored a leaflet she happened to read at the university, confronting Hans with her knowledge, and asking to be included in the resistance work. However, another of Sophie's sisters, Elisabeth Hartnagel-Scholl, cites evidence that Sophie came to Munich already fully informed about Hans's and Alexander's activities. Scholl and Sölle, 32–34; Chaussy and Ueberschär, 143.

68. Sophie Scholl, letter to Lisa Remppis, November 19, 1942, as quoted in *Briefe,* 508, n. 577.

69. Sophie Scholl, letter to Lisa Remppis, September 2, 1942, *Letters and Diaries,* 244.

70. Interview with Lilo Ramdohr in Sibylle Bassler, *Die Weisse Rose: Zeitzeugen Erinnern Sich* (Reinbek: Rowohlt, 2006), 131. Alexander's eagerness to exert himself in making others happy is manifested in a

letter written in 1942 after his return from Russia, where he was sent for several months to serve as a medical orderly. He is sending a young woman he had met there a watch as a Christmas gift. He apologizes that it is not a gold watch, as he had hoped to get for her, "but where can one find such a watch now? How long I've searched, until I was lucky enough to find this one … But, mind you, this one is Swiss, and these are the best in the world. As soon as I find a gold one, I will send it to you." Alexander Schmorell, letter to Nelly, end of November/beginning of December 1942, *Briefe*, 514.

71. *Freundschaften*, 55.

72. Sophie Scholl, letter to Lisa Remppis, January 14, 1942, *Letters and Diaries,* 189.

73. Inge Scholl's description in *Windlicht*, a private letter-magazine that circulated among the Scholls and their friends, to which they took turns contributing essays on culture and philosophy, as quoted in *Letters and Diaries*, 305–307, n. 179.

74. Sophie Scholl, undated draft of a letter, *Letters and Diaries,* 190.

75. Sophie Scholl, diary entry for July 15, 1942, *Letters and Diaries,* 208.

Chapter 5

76. Most of the letters Alexander wrote to Angelika in the spring of 1941 are signed "Alyosha."

77. The expression is from Hanser, *Noble Treason*, 116.

78. "Hochland," Harald Fischer Verlag, http://www.haraldfischerverlag. de/hfv/reihen/KLP/hochland_engl.php.

79. Thomas Molnar, "Thus spoke Bernanos," *Crisis Magazine*, April 1, 1986, http://www.crisismagazine.com/1986/thus-spoke-bernanos.

80. Claudel as quoted by Hans in a letter to Rose Nägele, February 16, 1943, *Letters and Diaries*, 279.

81. Hans used these words as an epigraph to an article he wrote on the Turin Shroud for *Windlicht. Letters and Diaries*, 167. This assertion is expressed in *The Satin Slipper*, Claudel's highly philosophical play of redemption and selfless love. The circle of friends read it together, with each taking a different role. Although Alexander hosted the reading at his home, he did not partake in the reading of the play. It seems the play did not move him as it did the others.

82. The books were returned to the monastery after the war by Hugo Schmorell.

83. Carl Muth as quoted in Hinrich Siefken, *Die Weisse Rose und ihre Flugblätter: Dokumente, Texte, Lebensbilder, Erläuterungen* (Manchester, England: Manchester University Press, 1994), 171.

84. Haecker's journal was published posthumously in German under the title *Tag- und Nachtbücher: 1939–1945.* Cited here is the English translation: Theodor Haecker, *Journal in the Night*, trans. Alexander Dru (New York: Pantheon Books, 1950).

85. Ibid., journal entry no. 487 (undated, early 1941).

86. Ibid., journal entry no. 583 (undated, late 1941).

87. Ibid., journal entry no. 217.

88. For some time, *Hochland* had published articles discussing the effects of the Russian Revolution, especially from the spiritual standpoint.

89. Hinrich Siefken, "'Die Weisse Rose' and Russia," *German Life and Letters* 47, no. 1 (1994): 14–43.

90. Ibid., 16.

91. Nikolai Berdyaev (1874–1948) turned from Marxism to Christianity through the influence of Jakob Boehme's mysticism, German idealism, and Dostoyevsky. He was a member of the Russian Orthodox Church, although he found himself at odds with some of its practices and teachings. Exiled from Russia in 1922 by the Soviet government, Berdyaev continued to write and publish his works in various European languages.

92. This and all following Berdyaev quotations are taken from his work *The End of Our Time* (also known as *The New Middle Ages*) as published in: Nicholas Berdyaev, *The End of Our Time: Together with an Essay on the General Line of Soviet Philosophy*, trans. by Donald Attwater (London: Sheed & Ward, 1935); published in German translation from the Russian in 1927, this work was read avidly by Hans and Christoph.

Chapter 6

93. Bishop von Galen, "Three Sermons in Defiance of the Nazis by Bishop von Galen," The Church in History Information Centre, http://www.churchinhistory.org/pages/booklets/vongalen(n).htm.

94. Ibid.

95. Ibid.

96. Hitler's order of August 28, 1941. Conway, *The Nazi Persecution,* 283.

97. Hanser, *Noble Treason,* 118.

98. Dumbach and Newborn, *Sophie Scholl,* 68.

99. *Freundschaften*, 51.

100. Lilo Ramdohr remembers a winter's day when Alex dragged her outside to make a snowman. *Freundschaften, 28.*

101. Hanser, *Noble Treason*, 146.

102. Hanser's expression, Ibid., 151.

103. Martin Bormann, Nazi party leader and Hitler's deputy, summed up the Nazis' attitude toward the Slavs in a memo dated August 19, 1942: "The Slavs are to work for us. In so far as we do not need them, they may die." Robert S. Wistrich, *Who's Who in Nazi Germany* (New York: Macmillan, 1982), 19.

104. The students had met Manfred Eickemeyer (1903–1978) through Professor Muth. Eickemeyer's studio became a venue for some of the group's reading evenings. Later, some White Rose leaflets were printed and stored in the studio's basement.

105. Interview with Nikolai Hamazaspian as quoted in Chaussy and Ueberschär, *Es Lebe Die Freiheit,* 124.

106. *Freundschaften,* 54.

107. Hanser, *Noble Treason*, 177.

108. Interrogations of Alexander Schmorell on February 25 and 26. Alexander Schmorell's interrogations, quoted and translated by me from pages 346–396 of Chaussy and Ueberschär, *Es Lebe Die Freiheit*, will be referenced by date rather than by page number. —*EP*

109. Susanne Hirzel, *Vom Ja Zum Nein: Eine Schwäbische Jugend 1933–1945* (Tübingen: Silberburg-Verlag, 2000), 182.

110. Scholl and Sölle, *The White Rose*, 30; Hanser, *Noble Treason*, 128, attributes this quote in a slightly truncated form to Alexander.

Chapter 7

111. Interrogation, February 26.

112. Siefken, *Die Weisse Rose und ihre Flugblätter*, 19.

113. Quoted in Hanser, *Noble Treason*, 168.

114. All excerpts from the White Rose leaflets quoted herein are cited from Dumbach and Newborn, *Sophie Scholl*, 186–205. For the full text

(in English) of the six leaflets, as well as Christoph Probst's draft of the seventh, online, see Katja's Dacha, "Leaflets of the White Rose," http://www.katjasdacha.com/whiterose/leaflets/index.html. The leaflets are appended to the books, cited herein, by Scholl and Sölle, *The White Rose*, and by Dumbach and Newborn, *Sophie Scholl*.

115. Christoph's words as quoted in Scholl and Sölle, *The White Rose*, 37.

Chapter 8

116. Jürgen Wittenstein took many of the photographs of the White Rose that have since become iconic—most notably of Sophie and Christoph bidding farewell to Hans, Alexander, and Willi at the Munich train station as they leave for duty in Russia.

117. Hubert Furtwängler, a nephew of the well-known conductor Wilhelm Furtwängler, and Alexander's friend, who sang with Willi in the Munich Bach Choir. He attended the group's evening readings in 1942–1943 and knew of the White Rose leaflets, but did not participate in their writing or dissemination. If Alexander, Hans, and Willi were missing at roll call in the Student Military Company, he would stand in for them, sometimes for all three on a given day, shouting 'Hier!' in a different voice for each one. Hanser, *Noble Treason,* 143.

118. Christoph Probst, as a family man, fulfilled his wartime duties in Germany.

119. First White Rose leaflet.

120. Willi Graf, diary entry, as quoted in Dumbach and Newborn, *Sophie Scholl*, 98.

121. Ibid., 99.

122. Alexander Schmorell, letter to his parents, August 5, 1942, *Briefe*, 495.

123. Hans Scholl, letter to his parents, August 7, 1942, *Letters and Diaries*, 215.

124. Alexander Schmorell, letter to Angelika Knoop, May 2, 1941, *Briefe*, 372.

125. Alexander Schmorell, letter to Lilo Ramdohr, August 7, 1942, *Briefe*, 498.

126. Alexander Schmorell, letter to his parents, August 28, 1942, *Briefe*, 501.

127. Willi Graf, diary entry, as quoted in Dumbach and Newborn, *Sophie Scholl*, 102. The medics spent many an evening reading Dostoyevsky by candlelight.

128. Later on, when Alexander returns to Germany, this fisherman will acquire a Romantic symbolism for him: "A fisherman, who sits far, far away somewhere in my distant homeland, cast his fishing line deep into my breast. And the further I went from my homeland, ... the stronger he tugged at his line, and the more woe filled my breast." Letter to Margaret Knittel, January 1943, *Briefe*, 520.

129. Alexander Schmorell, letter to his parents, August 5, 1942, *Briefe*, 495.

130. Hans Scholl, diary entry for August 9, 1942, *Letters and Diaries*, 224.

131. Hans Scholl, diary entry for August 28, 1942, *Letters and Diaries*, 235.

132. Ibid.

133. Alexander Schmorell, letter to his parents, October 10, 1943, *Briefe*, 503.

134. Alexander Schmorell, letter to his parents, October 17, 1943, *Briefe*, 504.

135. Ibid.

136. Willi Graf, diary entry for October 31, 1942, as quoted in *Letters and Diaries*, 243.

137. Robert Scholl had been denounced by his secretary to whom he had addressed his comment. After serving a sentence of four months, he was released but forbidden to practice law.

138. The leaflets, of course, had attracted the attention of the secret police, to whom copies were turned in by recipients. An investigation was launched. Yet, as Robert Mohr, the Gestapo investigator who interrogated Sophie Scholl and Will Graf, recounted later, "the investigation conducted to ascertain the originators [of the leaflets –*EP*] remained without result. Various circumstances suggested that the authors of the leaflets were to be found in Munich; however, for the time being, more precise clues were lacking." Robert Mohr, eyewitness account, in Inge Scholl, *Die Weisse Rose*: *Erweiterte Neuausgabe* (Frankfurt am Main: Fischer Taschenbuch, 1994), 171.

Chapter 9

139. The first bombing raid on Munich took place on October 30, 1942.

140. *Freundschaften*, 88.

141. According to parish records, membership had risen from approximately 250 in 1941 to more than 630 in 1942. These figures did not include people who attended services but were not registered parishioners. G. Seide, "Kafedral'nyi Sobor sv. Nikolaia v Miunkhene" [The Cathedral of St Nicholas in Munich], *Vestnik Germanskoi Eparkhii Russkoi Pravoslavnoi Tserkvi Za Granitsei*, 3 (1991): 23.

142. Leavened bread used in Orthodox Christian churches for the Eucharist.

143. The parish was founded in 1921, the very year that the Schmorell family fled from Russia and settled in Munich. Initially, services were held in rented spaces every two weeks by visiting clergy. In the late 1920s and early 1930s, however, there were periods in which services were held only on great feasts and Pascha, as the parish did not have a permanent rector. Seide, "Kafedral'nyi Sobor sv. Nikolaia," 23–24.

144. At this time, Fr Alexander (Andrei Lovchii; 1891–1973) was a monastic with the rank of hegumen; he became archimandrite in 1943. In 1945, he was consecrated vicar bishop of the German diocese of the Russian Orthodox Church Outside of Russia. He received the title "Bishop of Berlin and Germany" in 1951, and a year later was elevated to the rank of archbishop. Ibid., 24.

145. At first, the parish of St Nicholas did not have organized religious instruction for children. A Russian family, the Urtiews, moved to Munich in September of 1942; they asked Fr Alexander to give their two children lessons in the Law of God at his home. The brother and sister still remember him with great fondness: "Fr Alexander was an extraordinarily kind and loving person. After lessons he would often feed us. There wasn't much to eat in those days, but we would have a three-course meal: first—macaroni soup, followed by macaroni as a second course. And for dessert there would be macaroni sprinkled with sugar," remembers Eugenia Urtiew with a smile. Eugenia Urtiew, oral communication, March 20, 2015.

146. A study of Fr Alexander's sermons in *Voskresnyi Listok* has been published in Russian: E. Murzin, "V godinu tiazhkikh ispytanii: dukhovnaia zhyzn' i sotsial'no-politicheskaia problematika v propovediakh Arkhimandrita Aleksandra (Lovchego)" [In the hour of trial: The spiritual life and socio-political issues in the sermons of Archimandrite Alexander (Lovchii)], *Vestnik PSTGU II: Istoriia*. Moskva: PSTGU, no. 4, 65 (2015):

110–24. All excerpts from Fr Alexander's sermons quoted herein, as well as summaries of the sermons, have been paraphrased or translated by me from this source and will be referenced by the date of the sermon. —*EP*

147. November 28, 1943.

148. October 26, 1942.

149. November 22, 1942.

150. Ibid., December 20, 1942.

151. Ibid., September 27, 1942.

152. Ibid., October 4, 1942.

153. Ibid., May 28, 1944.

154. Ksenia Golenovsky Bogolubov, who was friends with Alexander at this time and also attended services at the parish of St Nicholas. Ksenia Golenovsky Bogolubov, oral reminiscences of Alexander Schmorell.

155. Alexander Schmorell, letter to Valia, November 25, 1942, *Briefe*, 511.

156. Alexander Schmorell, letter to Nelly, December 9, 1942, *Briefe*, 515.

Chapter 10

157. Earlier, Grimminger had come to the aid of the Scholl family by helping run Robert Scholl's practice while the latter was in prison.

158. Hanser, *Noble Treason*, 211.

159. Robert Mohr, eyewitness account, in Scholl, *Die Weisse Rose*, 171.

160. Lilo Ramdohr, eyewitness account, in Scholl, *Die Weisse Rose*, 140.

161. Interrogation, February 26.

162. Sophie uttered these words not long before her arrest. Wilhelm Geyer, eyewitness account, in Scholl, *Die Weisse Rose*, 168.

Chapter 11

163. A characteristic example is that of a man who was reported to the authorities for saying that the war was going badly for Germany. For this he was beheaded. Hanser, *Noble Treason*, 220.

164. Kurt Huber as quoted in Hanser, *Noble Treason*, 221.

165. Alexander Schmorell, letter to Nelly, December 9, 1942, *Briefe*, 515.

166. Alexander Schmorell, letter to Luise Hoferer, December 23, 1943, *Briefe*, 516.

167. Alexander Schmorell, letter to Margaret Knittel, January 1943, *Briefe*, 520.

168. *Freundschaften*, 102.

169. Lilo Ramdohr, eyewitness account, in Scholl, *Die Weisse Rose*, 143.

Chapter 12

170. Anne Nelson, *Red Orchestra: The Story of the Berlin Underground and the Circle of Friends Who Resisted Hitler* (New York: Random House, 2009), xxi–xxvi.

171. Many of these resisters would pay for their efforts with their lives.

172. Hanser, *Noble Treason,* 242. Information about what happened during Sophie's internment and interrogations—supplementary to her interrogation transcripts—was later written down by Robert Mohr, Sophie's interrogator, and Else Gebel, her cellmate. See Elsa Gebel's letter to the Scholl parents, written after the war, describing Sophie's final days in prison. It is appended to Scholl and Sölle, *The White Rose*,138.

173. Christoph was arrested in Innsbruck, where he was stationed, on Saturday, February 20, when he came to pick up his pay on the way to visit his wife, two small sons, and newborn daughter.

174. Leo Samberger, eyewitness account, in Scholl, *Die Weisse Rose*, 185.

175. Ibid., 184.

176. Dumbach and Newborn, *Sophie Scholl*, 157.

177. Ibid., 158.

178. This reflected Hans's firm conviction that the Nazis would soon fall and be brought to account for their evildoings. In the case of Freisler, however, Hans was wrong. Another kind of justice was meted out to him: he was killed in February 1945 by an Allied bomb during a trial in the People's Court in Berlin.

179. Leo Samberger, eyewitness account, in Scholl, *Die Weisse Rose*, 186.

180. Christoph's family found out about his arrest on the afternoon of Sunday, February 21, when the Gestapo arrived unexpectedly at the house of Christoph's mother in Tegernsee to confiscate a radio that Christoph had used in listening to foreign radio broadcasts. The family was not told on what grounds Christoph had been arrested, or when his trial would

take place. Only on Tuesday, February 23, did Herta Probst, Christoph's wife, receive the news of his death on the previous day from her father, Harald Dohrn, who softened the blow with the consoling words: "He has fallen on the right front." *Briefe*, 241, 252.

181. Christoph's death sentence bears eloquent testimony to Freisler's frenzied desire to physically wipe out any opposition to the Nazi regime. Christoph's only act of resistance known to the Gestapo had been to write the draft of a leaflet that had been neither duplicated nor disseminated. They also were aware that he had listened to foreign radio broadcasts. But he had not taken part in the printing or distribution of the leaflets, and he had not joined with his friends in painting anti-Nazi slogans.

182. Hanser, *Noble Treason*, 260.

183. Alexander later told the Gestapo that he found out about the arrest of the Scholls from a fellow student whom he happened to meet on a streetcar about an hour after Hans and Sophie had been arrested (Interrogation of Alexander Schmorell, February 26). This has given rise to the conjecture that Alexander was unaware of the Scholls's intended actions and was taken by surprise (Moll, *Briefe*, 253). Lilo Ramdohr, however, wrote that Alexander had volunteered to stand guard on the street at the entrance to the university while Hans and Sophie went inside and had watched events unfold (Lilo Ramdohr, eyewitness account in Scholl, *Die Weisse Rose*, 143–4).

Chapter 13

184. Lilo Ramdohr, eyewitness account, in Scholl, *Die Weisse Rose*, 145.

185. Of the works cited as sources for the White Rose chronology, the ensuing description of Alexander's flight and further ordeals draws most heavily on documentation provided in *Briefe* and *Freundschaften*. It is augmented by material from Khramov, *Russkaia Dusha*, who had the good fortune to personally interview Alexander's siblings, Erich and Natasha.

Chapter 14

186. Although the discharge was dated February 19, when Alexander was not yet arrested, it was nevertheless applied to him once he was taken into custody.

187. Only the answers given by the defendant are given in the interrogation transcripts of February 25 and 26. Questions posed by the interrogator and possible evidence with which Alexander was confronted are not presented, although they may be deduced at times.

188. This quotation and all subsequent quotations from Alexander Schmorell's interrogations are translated by me from his interrogation transcripts published in Chaussy and Ueberschär, *Es Lebe Die Freiheit*, 246–396.

189. Although the first part of the interrogation entitled "Personal Circumstances" takes up four pages of text in Chaussy and Ueberschär, *Es Lebe Die Freiheit*, this second part, entitled "To the Case," consists of twelve.

190. There is speculation that Alexander and Hans had agreed beforehand that they would both take full responsibility for all White Rose actions in case of arrest. See *Briefe*, 264.

191. Traute Lafrenz's contribution to the White Rose cause, in reality, was quite considerable. Thanks to the reticence of Alexander and the Scholls, the extent of her involvement was never established, and she received a comparatively "light" sentence of twelve months' imprisonment.

192. The transcript of this interrogation encompasses nearly eleven pages in Chaussy and Ueberschär, *Es Lebe Die Freiheit*.

193. Because, as Alexander maintained, Hamazaspian had not knowingly abetted him in his flight, he requested the Gestapo to return to Hamazaspian his jacket and fifty marks he had lent to Alexander, taking it out of the sum of money Alexander had on him at the time of his arrest. Hamazaspian had, however, provided the jacket and money specifically for Alexander's escape to Switzerland.

194. "*Ich bekenne mich zum Hochverrat, lehne es aber ab, mich auch landesverräterisch betätigt zu haben.*" Nazi law distinguished between high treason (*Hochverrat*), an attack against the state, and state treason (*Landesverrat*), an attack against a country involving a foreign government. Aside from denying that he had aided Germany's wartime enemies, perhaps Alexander also meant by this that he had not betrayed the true Germany.

195. Only six interrogation transcripts are extant in Alexander's case file. Moll, however, cites evidence of additional interrogations, possibly even after Alexander had already been sentenced to death. *Briefe*, 262.

196. Professor Huber's doctorate was declared null and void; he was divested of his status as university professor, leaving his wife and two children ineligible to collect his pension and, thus, destitute.

197. Falk Harnack as quoted in Dumbach and Newborn, *Sophie Scholl*, 168.

198. *Briefe*, 266.

199. Khramov, *Russkaia Dusha*, 161; *Briefe*, 268. Moll cites reports of gross physical mistreatment of Slavic prisoners by the Gestapo in Munich at this time.

Chapter 15

200. Siefken reports the fact the parent's meeting with Alexander without specifying a date. He also mentions that Erich Schmorell visited his brother in May, but he was not allowed to give Alexander a Russian Orthodox cross he had brought for him. Siefken, *Die Weisse Rose und ihre Flugblätter*, 136.

201. Hugo and Elisabeth Schmorell would receive a response of another kind (see chapter 15).

202. Khramov, *Russkaia Dusha*, 219.

203. Falk Harnack's narrative of the second White Rose trial is excerpted from his eyewitness account in Scholl, *Die Weisse Rose*, 152–63.

204. Susanne Hirzel's account of the trial is taken from Hirzel, *Vom Ja Zum Nein,* 218–34.

205. Susanne Hirzel describes it as being about the size of a classroom. Hirzel, *Vom Ja Zum Nein*, 221.

206. Dumbach and Newborn, *Sophie Scholl*, 173.

207. Hanser, *Noble Treason,* 271.

208. As the reason for this verdict, Freisler cited an extenuating circumstance: Falk was the only remaining son in the Harnack family. In reality, the Gestapo wanted to watch Falk in the hopes of tracing him to others in his executed brother's resistance group. Dumbach and Newborn, *Sophie Scholl*, 174.

209. Traute Lafrenz, eyewitness account, in Scholl, *Die Weisse Rose*, 135.

210. Ibid., 136.

211. *Briefe*, 275.

212. Hugo Schmorell may have known what Karl Alt, Protestant prison chaplain of Stadelheim from 1934 to 1945, revealed in 1946. "Because the release and burial of the bodies of executed prisoners (at the personal cost of the bereaved survivors) was denied in the case of 'political criminals' [i.e., those who disagreed with the regime —EP], these bodies were consigned to institutes of anatomy. When the latter had been filled to overflowing, the bodies were interred in mass graves, and received neither cross nor nameplate, with the result that the location of their final resting place could not be determined." Irene Stuiber and Jürgen Zarusky, *Hingerichtet in München-Stadelheim: Opfer Nationalsozialistischer Verfolgung Auf Dem Friedhof Am Perlacher Forst* [Executed in Munich-Stadelheim] (München: Landeshauptstadt München, Kulturreferat, 2004), 7.

213. Brinkmann, *Der Letzte Gang*, 101.

Chapter 16

214. The hymns of Great and Holy Monday, the first day of the week before Easter (called Pascha by Orthodox Christians), are quoted from Mother Mary and Archimandrite Kallistos Ware, *The Lenten Triodion*, South Canaan, Pa: St. Tikhon's Seminary Press, 1994, 511-21.

215. *Briefe*, 525, n629. Fr Brinkmann, who got to know Alexander well throughout the months of imprisonment, noted: "Schmorell professed the Russian Orthodox faith. For him, our faith was not warm-hearted, not loving enough. He was a fine, exceptionally well-read person, very interested in spiritual things." Brinkmann, *Der Letzte Gang*, 70.

216. Hanser, *Noble Treason,* 274.

217. Hirzel uses the expression *Sich-selber-Begegnen*—literally "self-encounter" or "self-confrontation." Hirzel, *Vom Ja Zum Nein*, 213.

218. The expression is Christoph Probst's, uttered by him years earlier.

219. Heb 11:34.

220. All but one of Alexander's letters from prison have survived only in copies made by Dr Hugo Schmorell. The originals perished in 1944 during an air strike. *Briefe*, 524.

221. The English translations of Alexander's letters from prison are taken from Helmut Gollwitzer, *Dying We Live: The Final Messages and Records of the Resistance* (New York: Pantheon, 1956), 55–58.

222. Death is not a subject that Alexander had broached in published letters that were written before his imprisonment. It is only from Lilo Ramdohr's recollections, dating to December 1942, that we learn that the topic had lately become a subject of interest for Alexander. Ramdohr wrote: "Our conversations [with Alexander] now centered on questions of faith, about attitude toward death … I would not and could not share the curiosity about the hereafter that Alex often exhibited. He, however, believed unwaveringly in a life after death." *Freundschaften*, 103.

223. The letter of June 5, is not included in Gollwitzer, *Dying We Live*, but has been translated by me from the German in *Briefe,* 526 —EP.

224. Hamazaspian's reminiscences as quoted in *Briefe*, 526, n631. The bicycle for the escape was to be provided by Alexander's friend, Konstantin Nikitin. The film *Sviatye* (*Saints*) contains an interview with ninety-one-year-old Nikitin who recounts the story (in Russian); http://5-tv.ru/programs/broadcast/507533/.

225. Theodore the Studite is likely meant.

226. Like Alexander's letter of June 5, the letter to Nelly is not included in Gollwitzer, *Dying We Live*, but has been translated by me from the German in *Briefe,* 527. According to Khramov, the letter was smuggled out by Fr Alexander (Lovchii) on the day he came to commune Alexander before his execution.

Chapter 17

227. In German, the phrase is *Eins vor allem lege ich Euch ans Herz*, more literally translated as "One thing above all I entrust to your hearts."

228. It is providential that Fr Alexander (Lovchii) was assigned full-time rector of St Nicholas's in August 1942. Prior to that date, it is doubtful that he, or any other Orthodox clergyman, would have been able to commune Alexander on such short notice.

229. In the original—"*Die letzte Tröstungen*," literally "the last comforts or consolation," a phrase used to refer to the last rites of the Roman Catholic Church.

230. Siegfried Deisinger, eyewitness account in Scholl, *Die Weisse Rose*, 192.

231. Ibid.

232. Deisinger as quoted in Hanser, *Noble Treason,* 276 (translation amended —EP).

233. This instrument of Alexander's martyric death is still in existence—a rare instance in the history of Christian martyrdom. The guillotine that was used for executions in Stadelheim Prison during the Nazi era was found and identified as such in early 2014. See Alison Smale, "A Guillotine in Storage Bears Signs of Role in Silencing Nazis' Critics," *New York Times,* January 10, 2014, http://www.nytimes.com/2014/01/11/world/europe/a-guillotine-in-storage-bears-signs-of-a-role-in-silencing-nazis-critics.html?_r=0.

234. Heb 11:13 [Paraphrased–*EP*]

235. Nearly twenty-six years earlier, Alexander's life in Christ had begun at his baptism in a church dedicated to the Apostles Peter and Paul.

236. Reminiscences of Alexander Schmorell by Nikolai Hamazaspian, Munich, 1989, as quoted in http://www.weisse-rose-stiftung.de/fkt_standard2.php?aktion=ls&ma=cs&c_id=mamura&id=11943878&page=1&topic=080&mod=10&lang=de.

Chapter 18

237. Interview with Elisabeth Hartnagel in Bassler, *Die Weisse Rose*, 29.

238. The narrative of the aftermath of the first two White Rose trials is compiled from the previously cited works of Chaussy and Ueberschär, *Es Lebe Die Freiheit*; Dumbach and Newborn, *Sophie Scholl*; Hanser, *Noble Treason*; Khramov, *Russkaia Dusha*; Scholl and Sölle, *The White Rose*; with the addition of Christian Petry, *Studenten aufs Schafott*.

239. The sixth White Rose leaflet, written soon after the short-lived outburst of protest occasioned by Giesler's speech, had hopefully called this incident at the University of Munich "the beginning of the struggle for our free self-determination."

240. Bishop Berggrav, Primate of the Church of Norway (Lutheran), was a leading figure in the resistance to the Nazi occupation of Norway during World War II.

241. Chaussy and Ueberschär, *Es Lebe Die Freiheit*, 514–5.

242. The words of an inmate of Auschwitz, as quoted in Hanser, *Noble Treason,* 282.

243. In the early 1930s, Mann had strongly denounced National Socialism in essays and public addresses. His German citizenship had been revoked in 1936 by the Nazi government. In exile, he taped a series of BBC radio addresses entitled *Deutsche Hörer!* (German listeners!).

244. Scholl and Sölle, *The White Rose*, 152.

245. The *New York Times* article of August 2, 1943, is appended in Dumbach and Newborn, *Sophie Scholl*, 226.

246. Scholl and Sölle, *The White Rose*, 159.

247. Hanser, *Noble Treason,* 285.

248. Scholl's *Die Weisse Rose*, first published in 1952 (with numerous subsequent editions and translations), fostered the memory of the White Rose. In 1954, Alexander's letters from prison were published in a compilation of letters written by inmates of Nazi prisons on the eve of their executions. Published first in German, this moving book by Gollwitzer came out two years later in English translation under the title *Dying We Live: The Final Messages and Records of the Resistance.*

249. The church is now dedicated to the Holy New Martyrs of Russia (glorified by the Russian Orthodox Church Outside of Russia in 1981), with a side altar in honor of St Nicholas.

250. He was glorified as a locally venerated saint of the Diocese of Berlin and Germany of the Russian Orthodox Church Outside Russia.

251. The service to St Alexander was composed by Archbishop Mark of Berlin. For the service in Slavonic, see http://sobor.de/images/stories/pdf/schmorell_sluzhba-2012.pdf. For a translation of this service into English, see "Month of June, the 30th Day, Commemoration of the Holy New-Martyr Alexander of Munich," http://orthodoxengland.org.uk/pdf/servs/alexander_of_munich.pdf.

252. For a lengthier description of the glorification, see Jim Forest, "A Canonization in Munich: Saint Alexander Schmorell," February 10, 2012, http://jimandnancyforest.com/2012/02/schmorell-canonization/.

253. "Speshyte Delat' Dobro!: Proslavlenie Muchenika Aleksandra Schmorelia," http://www.sobor.de/index.php?option=com_content&view=article&id=142%3Aa-canonization-in-munich-saint-alexander-schmorell&catid=79%3Aalexander-schmorell-verherrlichung&Itemid=109&lang=ru.

254. Alexander Solzhenitsyn, "Nobel Lecture in Literature (1970)."

Chapter 19

255. The third White Rose leaflet.

256. Conway, *The Nazi Persecution*, 259. For a full text of the circular see, Conway, *The Nazi Persecution*, Appendix 15, 383–86.

257. Conway, *The Nazi Persecution*, 299.

258. Helmuth James von Moltke and Beate Ruhm von Oppen, *Letters to Freya: 1939–1945* (New York: Vintage, 1995), 409.

259. Haecker, *Journal in the Night*, entry no. 300 (1940).

260. An example of this was the ruthless suppression of Christianity in the Warthegau area of annexed Polish territory. Conway, *The Nazi Persecution*, 311ff.

261. Cited in T. Schirrmacher, "National Socialism as Religion," Chalcedon Report (Patrick Henry College, 1992), http://www.phc.edu/gj_3_schirrmacher__ns__final.php.

262. As quoted in Conway, *The Nazi Persecution*, 103.

263. Sophie Scholl, letter to Fritz Hartnagel, May 29, 1940, *Letters and Diaries*, 69.

264. Lilo Ramdohr, eyewitness account, in Scholl, *Die Weisse Rose*, 140.

265. Chaussy and Ueberschär, *Es Lebe Die Freiheit*, 393–4. Alexander goes on to state his belief that for Russia "the only feasible form of government is monarchy. I do not mean to assert that this form of government as practiced before 1917 was my ideal—no. This monarchy, too, had shortcomings, perhaps even many—but fundamentally it was right. In the tsar, the Russian people had their advocate, a father whom they deeply loved, and with good reason. One saw in him not such much a head of state, but rather the father, provider, counselor of the people, and justifiably so, because such was the relationship between him and the people."

266. In pronouncing the sentence at the first White Rose trial, Judge Freisler had sneered contemptuously: "[Probst] is a 'nonpolitical man'— hence no man at all!"

267. Angelika Probst, address on February 22, 1946, as quoted in Robert Volkmann and Gernot Eschrich, ... *Damit Deutschland Weiterlebt! Christoph Probst (1919–1943)* (Gilching: Christoph-Probst-Gymnasium, 2000), 50.

268. Traute Lafrenz, eyewitness account, in Scholl, *Die Weisse Rose*, 131.

269. Josef Söhngen, eyewitness account, in Scholl, *Die Weisse Rose*, 123.

270. "And the Lord said to him, 'Go through the midst of the city, through the midst of Jerusalem, and put a mark on the foreheads of the men that sigh and that cry over all the abominations that are done within

it'." Ezek 9:4–6. The "mark" Augustine interprets as being the mark of Christ.

271. St Augustine, *Sermon 57 on the New Testament*. Translated by R.G. MacMullen. From Nicene and Post-Nicene Fathers, First Series, Vol. 6. Edited by Philip Schaff. (Buffalo, NY: Christian Literature Publishing Co., 1888). Revised and edited for New Advent by Kevin Knight. http://www.newadvent.org/fathers/160357.htm.

272. The White Rose circle was not alone in such sentiments. In a letter to his wife on November 6, 1941, Helmuth von Moltke railed against those people who find it comfortable to "deliberately wear blinkers that prevent one from seeing the evil done in the discharge of [their] responsibility—to be unwilling to see that one is [thus] defending murder and robbery. In reality, it is these people who are the crux of the evil, not the criminals. There are and have been criminals everywhere; but it is the inescapable duty of all the righteous to keep crime within bounds, and whoever evades this task is more guilty than the criminal himself." von Moltke and von Oppen, *Letters to Freya*, 178. Acting upon his convictions, von Moltke was imprisoned, sentenced to death by the People's Court, and hanged in January 1945 at the age of thirty-seven.

273. St John Chrysostom, *Homilies on Genesis*, Homily 17.

274. Solzhenitsyn, "Nobel Lecture."

275. Professor Huber thus expressed the motive of the White Rose at his trial. Hanser, *Noble Treason,* 167.

276. St Alexander's final letter from prison.

Chapter 20

277. Angelika Probst as quoted in *Briefe*, 278.

278. Col 3:9–10.

279. St Isaac the Syrian, *Ascetical Homilies*, Homily 5., in: *The Ascetical Homilies of Saint Isaac the Syrian*, Boston, Mass: The Holy Transfiguration Monastery, 1984.

280. The most striking example of Alexander's care for others is the concern for his family that he expresses in his final letters from prison. It might be expected that a person undergoing his ordeal might have put himself in the center of attention, yet his primary concern is to comfort and console his loved ones.

281. Metropolitan Hilarion's greeting on the occasion of St Alexander's canonization; "The First Hierarch Congratulates Archbishop Mark of Berlin and Germany, Bishop Agapit of Stuttgart, Clergy and Flock of the German Diocese and Participants in the Canonization of New Martyr Alexander Schmorell," February 3, 2012, the Russian Orthodox Church Outside of Russia, http://www.synod.com/synod/eng2012/20120203_print_engermandiocese.html.

282. Hieromonk Seraphim (Rose), "Forming the Soul—Spirit, Soul and Body," *Orthodox America* 19, vol. II, no. 9 (May 1982), http://www.roca.org/OA/19/19f.htm. Fr Seraphim asserted that "in general, the person who is well-acquainted with the best expressions of human art, literature and music—which in the West almost always have definite religious and Christian overtones—has a much better chance of leading a normal, fruitful Orthodox life than someone who knows only the popular culture of today."

283. Heb 13:14. [Paraphrased–*EP*]

284. One is reminded, however, of C. S. Lewis's dictum that "there are no *ordinary* people. You have never talked to a mere mortal. Nations, cultures, arts, civilizations—these are mortal, and their life is to ours as the life of a gnat. But it is immortals whom we joke with, work with, marry, snub, and exploit—immortal horrors or everlasting splendors." C. S. Lewis, "The Weight of Glory," in C. S. Lewis and Walter Hooper, *The Weight of Glory, and Other Addresses* (New York: Collier Books, 1980), 19.

Appendix 2

285. Seide, "Kafedral'nyi Sobor sv. Nikolaia," 24.

286. Russian Easter bread.

LIST OF ILLUSTRATIONS

1. Photographer unknown, Alexander Schmorell with his parents Dr Hugo and Elisabeth Schmorell and his siblings Erich and Natalia, ca. 1930, Family Schmorell. Scan of photograph, author archive. Source: Igor Khramov *Russkaia Dusha Beloi Rozy* [The Russian Soul of the White Rose], (Orenburg: Usadba, 2009).

2. Photographer unknown, Alexander Schmorell with Feodosia Konstantinovna Lapschina, ca. 1935, Family Schmorell. Scan of photograph, author archive. Source: Igor Khramov *Russkaia Dusha Beloi Rozy* [The Russian Soul of the White Rose], (Orenburg: Usadba, 2009).

3. Photographer unknown, Alexander Schmorell, 1939, Familie Schmorell. Scan of photograph, archive of Jim Forest. Source: https://www.flickr.com/photos/jimforest/sets/72157625346459536.

4. Photographer George J. Wittenstein, Alexander Schmorell at Munich University, 1940. Scan of photograph, archive of Jim Forest. Source: https://www.flickr.com/photos/jimforest/sets/72157625346459536.

5. Photographer Alexander Schmorell, Sculpted bust of Beethoven by Alexander Schmorell. Scan of photograph, author archive. Source: Igor Khramov *Russkaia Dusha Beloi Rozy* [The Russian Soul of the White Rose], (Orenburg: Usadba, 2009).

archive. Source: https://www.flickr.com/photos/jimforest/6831856543/in/photostream/.

18. Photographer Jim Forest, Schmorell Grave, August 22, 2006. Photographer's own archive. Source: https://www.flickr.com/photos/jimforest/5360867669/in/album-72157625346459536/.

19. Photographer Jim Forest, Schmorell canonization: Schmorell canonization: procession to the cemetery, February 4, 2012. Photographer's own archive. Source: https://www.flickr.com/photos/jimforest/6832007947/in/photostream/.

20. Photographer Jim Forest, Schmorell canonization: Prayer at the grave of Alexander Schmorell, February 4, 2012. Photographer's own archive. Source: https://www.flickr.com/photos/jimforest/6831856543/in/photostream/.

21. Photographer Jim Forest, Schmorell canonization: reception after the Liturgy, February 5, 2012. Photographer's own archive. Source: https://www.flickr.com/photos/jimforest/6831856543/in/photostream/.

22. Photographer Jim Forest, Schmorell canonization: the icon-bearing procession, February 4, 2012. Photographer's own archive. Source: https://www.flickr.com/photos/jimforest/6831856543/in/photostream/.

23. Photographer Jim Forest, New Martyrs, including Alexander Schmorell, February 21, 2009. Photographer's own archive. Source: https://www.flickr.com/photos/jimforest/6831856543/in/photostream/.

24. Photographer Jim Forest, Schmorell text, April 25, 2010. Photographer's own archive. Source: https://www.flickr.com/photos/jimforest/6851981917/in/album-72157629206699911/.

25. Photographer Jim Forest, Schmorell canonization icon, February 8, 2012. Photographer's own archive. https://www.flickr.com/photos/jimforest/6841477919/in/album-72157629206699911/.

INDEX